D1110331

The Financiers of Congressional Elections

Power, Conflict, and Democracy: American Politics Into the Twenty-first Century

Power, Conflict, and Democracy:
American Politics Into the Twenty-first Century
Robert Y. Shapiro, Editor

This series focuses on how the will of the people and the public interest are promoted, encouraged, or thwarted. It aims to question not only the direction American politics will take as it enters the twenty-first century but also the direction American politics has already taken.

The series addresses the role of interest groups and social and political movements; openness in American politics; important developments in institutions such as the executive, legislative, and judicial branches at all levels of government as well as the bureaucracies thus created; the changing behavior of politicians and political parties; the role of public opinion; and the functioning of mass media. Because problems drive politics, the series also examines important policy issues in both domestic and foreign affairs.

The series welcomes all theoretical perspectives, methodologies, and types of evidence that answer important questions about trends in American politics.

The Financiers of Congressional Elections

Investors, Ideologues, and Intimates

Peter L. Francia, John C. Green, Paul S. Herrnson,
Lynda W. Powell, and Clyde Wilcox

Columbia University Press   New York

Columbia University Press
Publishers Since 1893
New York   Chichester, West Sussex

Copyright © 2003 Columbia University Press

Library of Congress Cataloging-in-Publication Data
The financiers of congressional elections : Peter L. Francia . . . [et al.].
    p.   cm.—(Power, conflict, and democracy)
  Includes bibliographical references and index.
    ISBN 0-231-11618-7 (cloth : acid-free paper)—ISBN 0-231-11619-5
(pbk. : acid-free paper)
    1. Campaign funds—United States. 2. United States. Congress—
Elections—Finance. I. Francia, Peter L. II. Series.

JK1991.F55 2003
324.7'8'0973—dc21

2003048483

Columbia University Press books are printed on
permanent and durable acid-free paper.

Printed in the United States of America

c 10 9 8 7 6 5 4 3 2 1
p 10 9 8 7 6 5 4 3 2 1

Contents

Preface

Nothing is more important in the life of a democratic nation than its elections, and no issue is more controversial in American elections than the role of money. This book is about individuals who give significant contributions to congressional candidates. Although they provide a substantial portion of the money these candidates raise and spend, significant donors have up until this point been the subject of little scholarly investigation.

The genesis of this book dates back to the musings of three friends over a few beers just a few blocks from the U.S. Capitol. Shortly after the 1990 elections, Bob Biersack, Paul Herrnson, and Clyde Wilcox were discussing the likely impact of redistricting on the flow of money in congressional campaigns. We were able to speculate on changes in the flow party and PAC money but soon came to the conclusion that, before we could even begin to guess about the impact of redistricting on individual contributions, we would have to learn more about those who made them. We began the project in 1992 and labored over it on and off for several years. Over time, the personnel on the project changed. Bob had to drop out of the research team because the demands of his position at the Federal Election Commission became too great. John Green came on board and had a major hand in administering the survey on which much of the book is based. Lynda Powell joined the group and provided data for 1978 congressional contributors, as well as substantial expertise in data analysis. Peter Francia began working on the project as Paul Herrnson's graduate research assistant, but as he became more active in it he became a coauthor.

In the course of writing we incurred a number of intellectual debts. First and foremost, we owe Bob Biersack enormous thanks. Without his early efforts this project would not have been possible, and his continued support improved the book immensely.

Second, we thank various research assistants, including Peter Burns, Michael Gusmano, and Atiya Kai Stokes at the University of Maryland; Rachel Goldberg, Wesley Joe, and Ben Webster at Georgetown University; and Nathan Bigelow, who assisted both at the University of Akron and the University of Maryland. We also wish to thank the Center for Responsive Politics and James Snyder of the Massachusetts Institute of Technology for sharing data with us.

This project also benefited from the financial support of the Joyce Foundation and the encouragement of its vice-president, Larry Hanson. Additional funding was provided by National Science Foundation grants SES-9210169 and SES-9209342, which were awarded to Paul Herrnson and Clyde Wilcox. Support from the Dirksen Congressional Center provided Clyde Wilcox with graduate assistance. Funding from The Pew Charitable Trusts freed up Paul Herrnson and Peter Francia to devote additional time to the research. The Center for American Politics and Citizenship at the University of Maryland, the Ray C. Bliss Institute at the University of Akron, and the departments of political science at Georgetown University and the University of Rochester provided substantial staff assistance and support for the project.

We wish to thank David Diefendorf, Anne McCoy, and Michael Haskell of Columbia University Press. Special thanks go to John Michel, senior executive editor at Columbia Press, who was encouraging and patient, and who gave us a swift kick in the pants when we needed it. If ever an editor played a critical role in moving along a project, it was John.

The Financiers of Congressional Elections

chapter 1

Introduction

A thousand well wishers filled the Grand Ballroom of New York City's historic Puck Building on short notice three months ago for the bris of Charles Kushner's eight-day-old grandson. Rudy Giuliani was there. Former U.S. Senator Frank Lautenberg came. New Jersey's Governor McGreevey even managed to hobble in on crutches. The high-wattage turnout at the gala Jewish circumcision ceremony was no surprise to political insiders. Although far from a household name, the 48-year-old Kushner—a multimillionaire New Jersey real-estate developer—is renowned as a generous donor. . . . Kushner, his family, and business associates funneled at least $3.1 million to political committees and politicians. Kushner's four children gave almost $300,000, some even before they were old enough to vote. On a single day in March last year, Kushner's contribution network gave $237,000 to the state Democratic Committee. . . . Lautenberg, who has known Kushner for more than 20 years, compares the developer's family to legendary American families who have made their mark, such as the Rockefellers and Kennedys. Like them, Lautenberg said, Kushner aggressively promotes his philanthropic and political causes while advancing his business and personal interests.
—*The Record,* June 16, 2002

News stories about "fat-cat" donors such as Kushner, taken from the *The Record* of northern New Jersey, are among the most enduring images of American politics. From the "robber barons" of the gilded age to the "corporate rich" of the mid-twentieth century to the "Hollywood jetset-ters" who gave huge amounts of "soft money" during the last days of the twentieth century, fat cats have a firm place in the mythology of American politics. These legendary figures are frequently demonized—and occa-sionally lionized—for supposedly pulling the strings that control the ac-tions of members of Congress (Domhoff 1983). Fat cats and the business interests that they usually represent are often seen as part of the constella-tion of "special interests" that conspire to purchase "the best Congress money can buy" (Jackson 1988; Stern 1988).

Since academics first began to study this subject, rich contributors have been said to dominate campaign finance and exercise inordinate political power (Mills 1956; Nichols 1974; Dumhoff 1998; Allen and Broyles 2000). During the early days of the twentieth century, fat-cat donors to both the Republican and Democratic parties came from business interests, with banking, manufacturing, mining and oil, railroad and public utility, and re-tail businesses leading the way (Overacker 1932). Businesses continued to provide most of the funds for national elections in the middle of the centu-ry, but labor also played an important role (Heard 1960). In most cases, these contributors were perceived to be making contributions in order to win backing for policies that would help their company or union.

But campaign contributors do not always fit this stereotype. Although some contributors hope to win policy favors in exchange for their dona-tions, many give for other reasons. The financiers of congressional elec-tions include some individuals who give large amounts to many candidates in each congressional election, others who give smaller contributions to a few candidates in some elections, and still others who only occasionally give to a congressional candidate. Despite differences in the amounts they give, many of these donors have things in common—they are mostly white, male, and wealthy (Berg et al. 1981). They may, however, differ in their motives and political views. The following accounts of two fundrais-ing events are a composite of many stories told to us by significant donors that illustrate this diversity.

The fundraising dinner in Chicago was drawing to a close. Waving to the crowd, the congressman stepped off the platform to mingle with his guests, who had paid $250 to attend.

Tom Smith, a retired insurance agent and part-time lobbyist for his indus-try, immediately approached the congressman. He introduced his business associ-

ates seated at the same table. The congressman knew that most were Republicans, like Smith, and some clearly felt out of place at the Democratic candidate's event. After a few pleasantries, Smith confirmed an appointment for the following week.

A few moments later, the congressman was warmly greeted by an old friend, Dick Jones. A broadcaster by profession, Jones rarely missed an opportunity to socialize with the congressman, whom he had known since boyhood. In fact, he was well acquainted with many of the other attendees, and he was constantly interrupted by common well-wishers.

The congressman's aide pointed to another guest, Harriet White. A lawyer and environmental activist, she was anxious to discuss a clean water bill recently introduced in Congress. The congressman listened to a brief discussion of the bill's merits as well as some pointed advice about the upcoming campaign. To buttress her argument, White introduced Merrill Washington, a widower with no interest in politics but intense feelings about the local sewage treatment plant. After thanking them both, the congressman continued to work the crowd.

Meanwhile, half a continent away, another congressman stood just inside the Governor's Room in the Capitol Hill Club in Washington, D.C., welcoming attendees to a late-night cocktail party. A line of lobbyists, party leaders, and other politicians shook his hand, exchanged a few pleasantries, and then moved on.

Outside the room was a long table covered with name tags that read like a Who's Who of the Washington power structure. Representatives of the Mortgage Bankers Association, the Sugar Growers, McDonnell Douglas, J.P. Morgan, Travelers Insurance, NationsBank, Bell South, Florida Power, the American Medical Association, Gulf Power, American Community Bankers, and the National Rifle Association were all expected to be in attendance. The names of several prominent party and congressional leaders were evident as well.

The congressman knew many of his guests by name, but an aide stood at his ear to supply missing information. Most of the attendees had business before the subcommittee the congressman chaired. Others knew he might face a tough reelection campaign and wanted to help maintain Republican control of Congress. Many appreciated his staunchly conservative views. A few dropped a $1,000 check into a wicker basket beside the nametags. Most had paid in advance. An unexpected guest surprised the congressman: a major party fundraiser with a reputation for backing rising stars in Congress. The fundraiser introduced his partner, a prominent Democratic lawyer who had once served in the White House. As they turned to leave, the fundraiser and lawyer asked the congressman if he would like to join them for lunch "sometime after November." The congressman agreed and nodded for his aide to note the engagement before greeting his next guest.

These donors are more typical of the "significant donors" to congressional campaigns—individuals who gave at least $200 to at least one candidate in one campaign. Tom Smith is a typical "investor." He contributes to advance or protect his business interests. Harriet White gives for reasons of political principle. Like most "ideologues" she gives because she cares about important issues and causes facing the country. Dick Jones is an "intimate." He enjoys mingling with the friends, colleagues, and politicians who populate the world of congressional fundraising.

All three individuals are engaged in a rare type of political participation. Only a small portion of the public gives to congressional candidates—or indeed to any type of candidate or political group (Wilcox 2001). For example, in 1996 only about one-eighth of adults reported making a donation of any kind, and only one-half of those gave to a candidate for office (Rosenstone et al. 1997). Congressional candidates raised just a fraction of these donations, estimated to come from between two and four million people per election (Sorauf 1988).

And even among this small number who give to congressional candidates, few make significant contributions. The average size of a political contribution is less than $75—far less than the $200 threshold that requires a candidate to report the contribution to the Federal Election Commission (FEC) (Verba, Schlozman, and Brady 1995). In 1996, the Center for Responsive Politics estimated that some 370,000 individuals made contributions of $200 or more to congressional candidates.[1] This would mean that fewer than 0.2 percent of American adults donated enough money to a congressional campaign to legally require disclosure. Only a small portion of that percent made large contributions to many candidates. In 1990, the top 1 percent of individual donors—who constitute .00002 percent of citizens—provided 10 percent of all individual contributions to congressional candidates (Wilcox et al. 1998).

Despite their small numbers, individual donors play a critical role in financing congressional elections. Individual contributions typically account for more than half the money raised in House campaigns. Significant individual contributions—equal to $200 or more—comprise roughly two-thirds of all individual donations to congressional candidates. During the 1996 elections, Democratic and Republican House candidates in two-party contested races raised almost $178.2 million in significant individual contributions, accounting for approximately 36 percent of their total receipts.[2] Major-party Senate candidates raised almost $124 million, nearly 41 percent of their campaign war chests. The total in significant individual contributions raised by House and Senate candidates who made it into the general election was about $158.8 million and $95.6 million, accounting for roughly 36 percent and 43 percent of these candidates' receipts. Although the specific amounts raised from individuals in amounts of $200 or more typically increase from one election to the next, they consistently account for more than one-third of the money raised by congressional candidates (Herrnson, 2000).

The Role of Individual Donors

During the last decade the role of money and politics in general, and of large contributions in congressional elections in particular, has been the subject of roiling debate. The House passed several campaign finance reform bills over the vehement objection of the Republican leadership, only to face vigorous filibusters and ultimate defeat in the Senate (see Dwyre and Farrar-Meyers 2000). Then, the Senate finally passed a bill which immediately sparked heated debate and opposition in the House. Ultimately, the Bipartisan Campaign Finance Reform Act of 2002 (BCRA) was passed in both Houses of Congress and signed into law by the President, only to be immediately challenged in the courts by plaintiffs from both the left and right.

Proponents of BCRA, and of reducing the role of money in politics, argue that campaign contributing is *undemocratic* because the wealth of a few citizens can overwhelm the voices of the many. This criticism reflects two concerns. First, contributing is *unrepresentative*: donors have different views from those of the rest of the citizenry and their money allows them to express these views. Thus, contributing can distort the democratic process, leading government officials, including members of Congress, to misperceive the will of their constituents (Verba et al. 1995). Second, campaign contributing is *unprincipled*: donors are narrowly self-interested, instrumental in their behavior, and oblivious to the public interest. Many observers thus view campaign contributions as a form of corruption (Berg et al. 1976; Drew 1983).

Critics of the campaign finance system argue that contributions are made by an exclusive and unrepresentative elite that receives special access to policymakers. The spiraling costs of congressional campaigns means that members of Congress spend increasing amounts of time meeting with donors and potential donors, often in social settings such as fundraising events. Members are therefore far more likely to hear the voices of donors than of those who do not make contributions. If donors have a distinctive social profile (for example, if they are far wealthier than most Americans), or if they hold distinctive policy views (for example, if they are more likely to support tax cuts for the wealthy), then the process of political contributing can create representational distortion. Contributing is believed to be an especially serious source of this type of distortion (Constantini and King 1982; Verba et al. 1995).

Further, proponents of reform consider donors to be corrupters of American politics (Berg et al. 1976). Donors are often depicted as offering contributions in exchange for favors for their businesses or unions, and often winning special treatment in the tax code, special language in government rules regulating business, and special government appropriations in exchange for their "investments." Public policy is thus skewed to favor wealthy donors over average citizens who do not make contributions (Olson 1971; Stern 1988; Clawson et al. 1992; McChesney 1997; Gierzynski 2000).

The idea that contributions might be offered in exchange for policy favors—i.e., "quid pro quo" arrangements—was part of the U.S. Supreme Court's reasoning in upholding contribution limits on individuals and groups in the *Buckley v. Valeo* decision of 1974. The Court referred to "the real or imagined coercive influence of large financial contributions on candidates' positions," implying that donors can insist that politicians support their positions if they give them money. It ruled that corruption and the appearance of corruption associated with large campaign contributions were sufficiently serious problems to justify limiting contributions, despite claims that they are a form of political speech.

There is substantial evidence that the public does think of individual contributions—especially large contributions and those coordinated by interest groups—as a corrosive influence on democracy. Surveys show that a majority of Americans believe that contributions are often given in an effort to win political favors. They also believe that contributions influence policymakers. A *Washington Post* poll in 1997, for example, found that three-fourths of all Americans believed that members of Congress would vote the way their contributors wanted rather than voting their personal conscience at least half of the time.

Congressional reformers often liken large contributions to bribery, wherein a contributor buys the votes of a member of Congress. But often it is the member who asks for the contribution and the donor who feels compelled to comply. This process, by which members of Congress solicit contributions from donors, is often referred to as "rent seeking" (McChesney 1997). Incumbents are in a special position to ask certain potential donors for cash, for they routinely consider legislation that affects businesses, unions, and individuals. Many donors believe that the invitation is one they cannot refuse. Nonincumbents are usually unable to directly influence public policy and thus are less able to "extract rents."

Some observers take a very different view from that of the critics. Those who defend individual contributors argue that these individuals are active participants in politics. Donors do exactly what civic advocates and political theorists have long claimed good citizens should do: they contribute their money, skills, and time to the political process. In an era when few Americans are engaged in public affairs, these people show unusual public-spiritedness. Giving money is merely one additional form of political participation, and rather than bemoan the narrow contributor base, they argue, we should seek to expand and broaden that base. Those who give to candidates are likely to have a greater interest in following the candidate's behavior, and may learn about politics in the process. Contributing may well have positive benefits to donors (Wilcox 2001).

In addition, individual contributions provide candidates with important funds that help them to communicate their messages to voters. Individuals who make large contributions can provide seed money that candidates of modest means can use to raise more funds (Biersack, Herrnson, and Wilcox 1993), or they can serve as patrons for unpopular causes that enrich the political debate (Winter 1973). Moreover, individual donors help to dilute the impact of organized interests in financing elections. Although some donors give in coordination with organized interests, many do not. Thus significant donors provide a larger and more diverse funding source than would result if candidates were forced to rely entirely on groups. Donors have other motives, they argue, than merely personal gain. Some donors give to help elect candidates who share their views on the environment, gun policy, or abortion, and others give as part of a broader pattern of civic involvement (Brown, Powell, and Wilcox 1995).

Finally, some defenders of individual contributors argue that all citizens are entitled to give money to candidates and causes that they support because these contributions are a logical extension of freedom of speech. Candidates and parties cannot communicate their messages without money, and when individuals give to candidates they essentially help that candidate speak for the causes on which the contributor and candidate agree. Large contributions are merely the equivalent of shouting out that speech.

The debate over the role of money in politics and campaign finance reform involves two principles that are at the foundation of American government: liberty and equality (Mutch 1988; Ackerman 1993; Gierzynski 2000). The tradition of spending money to promote public policies and the political careers of those who share one's views is consistent with the concept of liberty espoused by English political philosopher John Locke and the founders of the United States. Individuals who hold this view maintain that liberty entitles individuals to use their wealth to promote their interests. The Declaration of Independence refers to the unalienable rights of life, liberty, and the pursuit of happiness. Locke and the founders understood wealth to be one of the most important means for pursuing happiness. They believed individuals should be free to spend their money as they see fit, including spending it to promote their preferred public policies. Centuries later, the U.S. Supreme Court took the argument a step further, equating spending money in politics with free speech.

Nevertheless, the right to spend money to pursue personal happiness is not without restrictions. Rights often clash. Democratic governments routinely limit individuals' and organized groups' economic, social, and political activities in order to protect others' freedoms and the national interest. Government regulations, particularly those concerned with elections, have been justified in the name of equality. Those who favor limiting the role of money in politics believe limits on campaign contributions and spending are needed to prevent the wealthy from amassing too much influence in elections and in policymaking in general. They argue that elections are the one part of our political process in which all should have equal input. Wealthy donors should not be able to dominate political discussion; policymakers should also hear the political perspectives of those of modest means. The financing of elections should not result in campaigns in which it appears to voters that one candidate shouts with a bullhorn and another is reduced to a mere whisper. The legislative process, administrative rule making and implementation, and even the courts are arenas in which wealthy and well-organized individuals and interests can use their resources to advance their causes. The electoral process, in their view, should not be as skewed in favor of the wealthier elements of society.

Individual Donors and the Law

Individuals and groups that want to influence public policy focus primarily on Congress. The legislation, oversight, representation, public education, and outreach in which members of Congress engage have major implications for many individuals and groups, motivating them to petition one or more legislators. The organization and operations of Congress make the institution and its members focal points for lobbyists and others who are interested in public policy. Because members of Congress serve at the pleasure of their constituents and rely on private funding to finance their campaigns, raising money is an important component of their reelection campaigns. These circumstances create a relationship of mutual dependence among some members of Congress and those who help them finance their campaigns. The members rely, at least to some degree, for campaign contributions on individuals and groups that have an interest in how they perform their legislative duties. The individuals and groups rely, to some extent, on members of Congress to perform their legislative duties in ways that work to the donors' advantage.

The symbiotic nature of the relationships between members of Congress and significant donors has not been lost on the public or political reformers. American history is punctuated by periods of public protest against instances of corruption—real and perceived—by members of Congress and those who finance their campaigns (Thayer 1974). The period following the Watergate scandal—when the Committee to Reelect the President (Richard Nixon) used an illegal slush fund to finance the break-in at the Democratic National Committee Headquarters—resulted in a major public uproar and led to calls for reforming the financing of political campaigns. The result was the passage of the Federal Election Campaign Act of 1974 (FECA). In 1976 the U.S. Supreme Court reviewed the FECA, striking down portions but upholding others in *Buckley v. Valeo*.

The FECA limited individuals to a contribution of $1,000 per candidate for each phase of the election. Generally this limited donors to a maximum of $2,000 per candidate for the primary and general elections, although occasionally a candidate will also be involved in a runoff election, which raised the maximum to $3,000. Individuals could give up to $5,000 to each political action committee (PAC) in each year, up to $5,000 to state party committees, and $20,000 to a party's national organizations (national, congressional, and senatorial committees). The law set $25,000 as the ceiling for an individual's total contributions to federal candidates and the federal accounts of PACs and party committees in a given year. Individuals could make unlimited independent expenditures to help to elect or to defeat a candidate as long as those expenditures are made without the candidate's knowledge or consent (see, e.g., Corado et al. 1997).

Congress also required that candidates, parties, and PACs report the names, addresses, and occupations of individual donors of more than $200 to the FEC, which makes the information available to the public. There was no requirement to disclose contributions of less than $200. In weighing the potential for corruption and pragmatic considerations concerned with the day-to-day management of a campaign, Congress decided the burden of bookkeeping would be great and the chance of corruption small. But contributions of $200 or more were considered as sufficiently significant in size to merit public disclosure.

In upholding limits on contributions to candidates, the Supreme Court focused on the potential of these larger contributions to cause corruption and to create the appearance of corruption that would erode public confidence in democratic institutions. But by 1979 changes in the regulations and law allowed individuals and groups to contribute unlimited amounts of "soft money" to national and state political parties. These contributions were ostensibly to be used only for party building, for generic party advertising and voter mobilization, and for state and local candidates. However, by the 1996 elections, both parties used the money to help elect individual candidates for Congress and President. Thus individuals could give only a limited amount to parties and candidates directly for federal elections, but there were no limits on the amount that they could give to the party committees for other activities that directly affected those contests.

After decades of debate, Congress passed the Bipartisan Campaign Reform Act of 2002, which sharply limits the ability of individuals or groups to make soft-money contributions but also increases the limit for individual contributions. The new law allows individuals to give $2,000 to a federal candidate in each phase of the election—double what had been allowed under FECA. The law also increases the contribution limits to political parties, but not to PACs. Finally, the law bans soft-money contributions. Even before the law went into effect, it faced a strenuous challenge before the Supreme Court. On its face, the law would increase the importance of significant donors, while decreasing the impact of the "fat-cat" contributors who gave hundreds of thousands of dollars to the parties. Prior to 2002, though, federal law limited donors to contributions of no more than $2,000 to any congressional candidate who ran in both a primary and general election, and it required that any contribution of more than $200 be disclosed to the FEC.

STUDYING INDIVIDUAL CONTRIBUTORS

The fact that individuals directly contribute millions of dollars to candidates is important. Nevertheless, it understates their roles in the financing of elections. These contributors are the ultimate source of the money that PACs and parties give to candidates as well. As we will show in chapter 2, most of the individuals who give to congressional candidates also give at least occasionally to political parties or PACs. Thus this tiny set of activists plays a critical role in financing congressional candidates. As politicians, political advocates, and the public continue to evaluate the system of financing elections, it seems remarkable that so little is known about these donors.

There is a rich and varied literature on the institutional sources of campaign funds. These studies do not directly address contributions by individual donors, but they offer some preliminary insights into why and how individuals contribute to congressional candidates. Political parties are rational actors seeking to maximize their seats in Congress. The strategic calculus that flows from this leads them to contribute most of their money and other forms of campaign support to candidates in close races (Jacobson 1985; Herrnson 1989, 2000). This suggests that individuals with strongly partisan motivations may use the same strategic calculus—especially those who receive party mailings and take party cues when making campaign contributions.

Political action committees (PACs) follow some combination of two general strategies when they participate in electoral politics. These are often referred to as ideological and access-oriented. Those that follow ideological strategies seek to maximize the number of members of Congress who support the group's position on a few issues or on a broader range of issues. These groups behave similarly to political parties; they view elections as their primary opportunity to affect the composition of the government and shape public policy (Gopoian 1984; Eismeier and Pollock 1988; Humphries 1991). They typically contribute to candidates in close races (Eismeier and Pollock 1986), and they are often willing to support nonincumbents. Groups that follow access strategies, on the other hand, attempt to secure influence, or at minimum gain an audience with, elected officials (Herndon 1982; Sabato 1984; Langbein, 1986; Grenzke 1989; Magleby and Nelson 1990; Sorauf 1992; Austen-Smith 1995). These organizations contribute mainly to incumbents, especially those who are in a position to advance or hinder the group's ability to achieve its goals.

The research on PACs suggests that some individual donors contribute to candidates in close races in order to increase the number of legislators who share their view. It suggests that others may contribute strictly to incumbents in order to enhance the donor's influence on the policy-making process. Some individuals may give to different candidates for both sets of reasons. All three types of individual donors may give in coordination with or take cues from PACs and interest groups. Many such organizations send their members newsletters and actively seek to influence their members' contributions.

Yet, compared to the voluminous literature on parties, PACs, and donors, there is little systematic research on the motivations and strategies of individual congressional donors (but see Jones and Miller 1985). Individual contributors have a similar but richer mix of strategies for participation in politics than organizations (Wilson 1973). Some individuals participate in politics for material reasons; they seek particularistic benefits and contribute to influence the policymaking process in ways that help themselves or their businesses (Synder 1990; Baron 1994). Others contribute for the purposive goals of promoting specific issues and general ideologies they care deeply about (Rosenstone and Hansen 1993; Meirowitz and Wiseman 2001). Still other individuals are motivated by social and personal considerations, sometimes referred to as solidary concerns. These people may be friends with candidates or enjoy attending political events. However, they may respond to the request of a close friend to make a contribution, though they themselves have little interest in politics (Alexander 1962, 1966, 1971, 1979, 1992; Alexander et al. 1976; Alexander and Corrado 1994).

Studies of presidential donors show there is a pool of habitual donors who give in most presidential elections (Brown, Powell, and Wilcox 1995 see also Dunn 1972). These individuals provide the vast majority of contributions to candidates for presidential nominations. They contribute for material, purposive, and solidary reasons. Campaign professionals have learned to tap into donor motives when fundraising. Some of the insights from research on presidential contributors inform our expectations about individuals who contribute to congressional candidates.

However, Congress is a much different political institution from the Presidency in its organization, operations, and election methods. The regulations governing contributions to congressional and presidential campaigns are also very different, resulting in these two sets of candidates turning to different sources for their campaign finances. Most presidential-nomination candidates participate in the federal matching funds program, which places a premium on individual contributions of $250, and accept federal funding during the general election, which prohibits their campaigns from accepting donations from any source other than the federal government.[3] Aspirants to the Presidency rarely raise more than 1 percent of their funds from PACs (Wayne 1998). Congressional candidates, by contrast, realize their greatest financial benefits when they raise the maximum legal contributions from individuals, parties, and PACs both during the primary contests and the general election.

Finally, studies by political practitioners, and a few academics, show that well-packaged, incendiary, direct-mail appeals are successful in raising modest contributions from ideologues who have strong beliefs about ideologically charged issues (Godwin 1988). Upscale fundraising events that allow individual donors the opportunity to spend some quality time socializing with the candidate or some other celebrity are useful in raising larger donations. Recent experience demonstrates that the Internet also has potential as a fundraising vehicle.

The research on political parties, PACs, and presidential campaigns may provide some insights into the motives and behavior of individuals who make significant contributions to congressional candidates. Nevertheless, many questions need to be answered in order to have a full understanding of contributions and fundraising in congressional elections.

First, who contributes? Is there a pool of significant donors who routinely give contributions of at least $200 to congressional candidates? Do they "look like America" or are they a narrow, unrepresentative elite? Is the donor pool evolving over time in response to candidates' imperatives to raise more money from more individuals to fuel their campaigns? Have broader societal changes, such as the entry of women and minorities into politics and the workforce, affected the composition of the donor pool? How well integrated are donors into networks of social and political groups?

Second, how much do significant donors contribute and to how many candidates? Is the typical donor a prototypical fat cat who gives large contributions to many candidates? Or, does the typical donor contribute to just one or two candidates in a given election cycle?

Third, what motivates significant donors to contribute to congressional candidates? The media typically portray congressional donors as individuals who are seeking to gain some payoff in the legislative process. How many donors fit this pattern? How many contribute for other reasons? What are the donors' political views? How representative are they of the general public?

Fourth, how do campaigns entice individuals to give? How do they identify members of the donor pool who are most sympathetic to their candidate? What assets and liabilities do different types of candidates bring to the fundraising process? Who do they select to help them solicit funds? What kinds of pitches do campaigns use to get donors to part with their hard-earned dollars?

Fifth, who gives to whom? How do individual donors decide which candidates to support? Do investors, ideologues, and intimates respond to different types of appeals and contribute to different kinds of candidates? Which group of donors has a greater preference for incumbents? Which is more likely to take a chance on challengers? Do they all contribute to candidates in hotly contested races or do some give to shoo-ins or likely losers?

Sixth, are significant donors merely checkbook activists or do they seek to further amplify their voice in politics by contacting members of Congress and their staffs? More fundamentally, how many donors have personal relationships with their elected House member or senators, or know other members of Congress personally? How many donors write their representatives letters, call their legislative staffs, personally speak to the member, or even testify before members of the House and Senate? For what purposes do they communicate with the people's branch of the government? Is it primarily to seek personal favors, advance a political cause, or to socialize over drinks?

Finally, how do the donors feel about the campaign finance system in which they participate? Do they think the system works well or do they view it as deeply flawed? Do they share the general public's skepticism about donors buying access and members of Congress pressuring donors for support? What kinds of reforms are significant donors willing to support? Is there consensus among them about some reforms or are they as deeply divided on a partisan basis as are members Congress?

The answers to these questions have important implications for American politics. If the donor pool constitutes a rich, white, male elite that shares similar motives and political views, it could skew representation in Congress and distort the policymaking process. If, on the other hand, the donor pool looks like America and its members have diverse motives and political views then representational distortion will not be as severe. The answers to these questions also have important implications for the conduct of congressional campaigns. Some have asserted that congressional candidates wage a campaign for votes and a separate campaign for resources (Herrnson 2000). What are the implications of the campaign for resources as it is waged among significant congressional donors? This study is designed to address these issues and questions.

The Study

This research draws primarily on a large-scale survey of significant donors who gave at least $200 to at least one congressional candidate in 1996. It also relies on a smaller survey of major donors who contributed at least $8,000 to congressional candidates, and in-depth interviews with donors and with congressional campaign finance directors who worked on congressional campaigns. We supplement these data with information from the FEC on individuals' campaign contributions and candidates' receipts. We also collected information on candidates' backgrounds, including committee assignments and leadership assignments for incumbents, political experience for nonincumbents, and ideology for all candidates.

In addition, all of us have been involved to some extent in the fundraising process. We have all received personal, targeted, and untargeted contribution solicitations and attended fundraising events. One of us gained an insider's knowledge of the fundraising process—including how to organize a finance committee, put together a solicitation list, write a solicitation script, solicit prospective donors over the telephone, and organize a fundraising event—while working with a professional finance director to raise money for a congressional candidate. Our survey data, statistical analysis, in-depth interviews, and participant-observation have enabled us to provide a thick description of campaign contributors and the fundraising process.

The book is organized into eight chapters. Chapter 2 focuses on the social characteristics of congressional contributors, such as their socioeconomic status, gender, age, and race. We begin by investigating the critics' charges that contributors are a wealthy and homogeneous elite. We find that contributors are indeed overwhelmingly wealthy, highly educated, male, and white. The pool of congressional contributors does not remotely look like America, and thus concerns about the descriptive representativeness of donors are well founded. Most contributors are members of business groups and practically none are members of unions, but they also are members of a very diverse set of issue groups.

Donors' motives for giving and political attitudes are the subject of chapter 3. The popular stereotype that contributors are primarily wealthy businessmen who give in order to gain narrow economic advantage dramatically underestimates the diversity of the donor pool. Contributors give for many reasons—"investors" seek material gain; "ideologues" give in order to promote public goods, salient public issues, or some broad view of the good society; and "intimates" give because they enjoy personal and social relationships with candidates and other donors. More important, contributors hold divergent views on many political issues. Although most donors are very wealthy, many support increased spending on social welfare programs. Donors may sing with an upper-class accent, but they sing different songs.[4] Not every voice is represented among donors: there are few Christian conservatives, few union supporters, and no poor people.

Chapter 4 examines candidates, donors, and fundraising techniques. Candidates enter an election with different assets and liabilities. Potential contributors approach an election with various objectives and goals. The art of fundraising is to bring the two together. Fundraising professionals target those individuals most likely to respond to particular candidates, and they have developed a variety of solicitation techniques to appeal to different types of donors. This process reinforces the static composition of the donor pool.

Chapter 5 moves from the fundraising process to that process's major outcome. The first part of the chapter analyzes the factors that determine who gives to whom. The second part assesses the outcomes of those decisions in terms of which candidates benefit most from the system. Investors, ideologues, and intimates respond to different types of candidates, but incumbents are major beneficiaries of most campaign contributions.

Chapter 6 goes beyond contributing to investigate how congressional donors amplify their voices in the political system. Many contributors not only give money, they also contact members of Congress to express positions on policy. In chapter 7, we explore the contributors' perspectives on reforming the campaign finance system. Perhaps surprisingly, contributors of both parties are quite critical of the current system of campaign finance. They also are in considerable agreement on many of the specific reforms in the current debate. Democrats and Republicans alike favor a ban on soft money, favor limits on spending by congressional candidates, and even favor limits on TV advertising. But there are, to be sure, some party differences. Republicans, for example, are more likely to favor eliminating all contribution limits and requiring full disclosure than are Democrats. However, only a plurality of Republicans, not a majority, favors eliminating these limits. Thus, the differences between Republicans and Democrats are relatively modest, with the exception being a substantial difference of opinion on the public financing of campaigns.

In the final chapter, we summarize the book's major findings and place them into a broader context. We return to the normative concerns surrounding the influence of the financiers of congressional elections on American politics. We address questions concerned with the roles of significant donors and money in elections.

chapter 2

Who Are the Financiers of Congressional Elections?

Significant donors to congressional candidates are unusual and important actors in American politics. They are unusual because so few Americans make contributions of $200 or more to candidates. They are important because they provide a major portion of the funds collected by House and Senate candidates. They also form a core of citizens with whom candidates interact regularly. As campaigns have become more expensive, candidates have spent increasing portions of their time talking with and mingling with donors and asking them to give to their campaigns. If donors are an unrepresentative elite, or if their policy views are very different from those of the average citizen, then their special access to policymakers raises troubling questions about Americans' "voice and equality" in politics (Verba et al. 1995). There is little question that donors have a special voice in politics, and as we will see later in this book, most have ready access to members of Congress.

The increasing amounts of time that candidates spend talking with donors is troubling if these donors do not "look like America"—that is, if they have a distinctive demographic profile. Simply put, if a majority of donors are wealthy businessmen seeking policies to help their companies, then the messages that they give to candidates at fundraising events will not represent those of the average citizen. The special access of donors also would be more troubling if donors turn out to have policy views that are at odds with the majority of Americans.

When political activists have distinctive views and special access to policymakers, representation and democracy may become distorted. Political activists at all levels differ from nonactivists—voters are better educated and older than nonvoters, for example. But the representational distortion that comes from campaign contributions is especially large (e.g., Verba et al. 1995). In part, this is because income is more concentrated in America than is free time. Citizens at all income levels might find time to work for a candidate, but only the wealthiest can afford to give $200 or more. In part the distortion arises from the fact that there are limits to the amount of time that can be volunteered—a day has only twenty-four hours for every citizen—but the potential amount of money that can be given is almost unlimited. Indeed, individuals can give an aggregate amount of $50,000 directly to the federal accounts of candidates, political parties, and PACs over the course of a two-year election cycle, unlimited amounts to the nonfederal (soft money) accounts of federal party committees, and unlimited amounts to state and local campaigns in more than a dozen states, depending on state law (Malbin and Gais 1998).

For these reasons, it is important to understand who gives money to political campaigns and what these people think about public policy. In this chapter we describe the donors' background characteristics and provide an overview of their political involvement, including their general patterns of contributing and working in campaigns and their involvement in interest groups. In the next chapter, we explore the motives and political views of donors.

THE DONOR POOL

There is an enduring pool of individuals who consistently make contributions in many elections. Some individuals consistently support presidential candidates, and they provide these candidates with a majority of their contributions of $200 or more (Brown et al. 1995). There is an enduring pool of significant donors to congressional candidates as well. More than half of all congressional donors give in most elections to House candidates, and more than 40 percent give in most elections to Senate candidates (see table 2.1). Fully 55 percent contribute in most elections to a House candidate, a Senate candidate, or both, and these donors provide a large portion of the candidates' campaign chests. There is even more evidence of the enduring nature of the donor pool: 53 percent of those who made congressional contributions in 1978 were still making contributions to congressional and presidential candidates, PACs, and party committees in the 1990s, despite the fact that 46 percent of them were over the age of 70 in 1996.[1]

TABLE 2.1. THE FREQUENCY OF MAKING A CAMPAIGN CONTRIBUTION TO CONGRESSIONAL CANDIDATES OR OTHER POLITICAL ORGANIZATIONS

	All	*Occasional*	*Habitual*
Gave to House candidates in:			
Most elections	51%	0%	92%
Some elections	43	91	5
Never	5	9	2
Gave to Senate candidates in:			
Most elections	41%	0%	74%
Some elections	48	85	18
Never	11	15	8
Gave to presidential candidates in:			
Most elections	39%	12%	60%
Some elections	37	55	23
Never	24	33	17
Gave to state or local candidates in:			
Most elections	48%	19%	71%
Some elections	40	64	20
Never	13	17	9
Gave to political party committees in:			
Most elections	31%	11%	48%
Some elections	38	51	28
Never	31	38	25
Gave to political action committees in:			
Most elections	24%	12%	34%
Some elections	29	34	25
Never	47	54	42
Gave in most elections to any source	72%	36%	100%
Did not give in most elections to any source	28	64	0
Gave in most elections to House or Senate candidate	55%	0%	100%
Did not give in most elections to House or Senate candidate	45	100	0
Gave in most elections to each type of candidate	23%	12%	100%
Did not give in most elections to each type of candidate	77	88	0
(N)	(960)	(427)	(533)

Note: Chi-Square tests indicate that all differences between occasional and habitual donors are statistically significant at p<.001. Some columns do not add to 100 percent due to rounding.
Source: The Congressional Donors Survey.

Many contributors also give in most elections to presidential and to state and local candidates. Nearly 40 percent of significant donors give to presidential candidates, and almost half give to a state or local candidate in most elections. Significant congressional donors not only give to candidates, many contribute to parties or PACs as well. More than 30 percent give to party committees and almost a quarter give to PACs in most elections. A large majority of congressional donors regularly contribute to different types of political campaigns. More than seven out of ten congressional donors give in most elections to at least one candidate, party committee, or PAC. In fact, almost one-quarter of all congressional donors state they contribute to House, Senate, presidential, state, *and* local candidates. Congressional donors are almost all members of a more general pool of people who give money to political campaigns: only 3 percent of these contributors say that they have never given to another type of candidate or committee. The financiers of congressional elections are often hyper-donors who help fund all types of candidates and groups at all levels of elections.

Occasional and Habitual Donors

There are important variations in giving among congressional donors. Some contributors—labeled "occasional donors"—report that they do not contribute to congressional candidates in most elections.[2] Rather, they contribute only in some elections, and often only when a friend runs for Congress or when a friend makes a solicitation on behalf of a candidate. Many of these individuals are probably only temporary members of the donor pool who are drawn in by personal factors. They contribute only as long as they have personal ties to a candidate or a fundraiser but later stop making contributions.

More than one-third of all occasional donors, however, give in most elections to some other type of candidate or political committee, most frequently to those involved in state or local races. This suggests the strength of personal ties in recruiting members of the donor pool. Many occasional donors begin to give to congressional candidates when a state or local candidate whom they have supported in the past runs for the House or Senate for the first time.

Over a period of time, some occasional donors become habitual donors. A fundraising industry has developed sophisticated tools to identify potential donors and to find the right appeals to induce them to contribute. This industry collects and organizes the names of new donors; it tries to persuade them to give more money to different candidates and to become regular members of the donor pool. As a result, new donors are likely to be asked to give again.

Other congressional contributors—labeled "habitual donors"—give in most elections to congressional candidates. They contribute in most elections to at least one House candidate, one Senate candidate, or more. Fully two-thirds of all habitual donors contribute to House, Senate, state, and local candidates in most election years. Many also contribute to parties and PACs. Habitual donors give more regularly to House candidates than state or local candidates; the opposite holds for occasional donors. There is a subset of habitual donors who make large contributions to many candidates. These so-called "major donors" constitute only 8 percent of all congressional contributors, but they receive the lion's share of media coverage. They provide slightly more than one-third of all contributions made by donors, but they are so few in number that it is difficult to generalize about them from our survey and interviews. Habitual donors, including major donors, constitute the low-lying fruit of fundraising; they are the ones to whom fundraisers turn first.

The distinction between occasional and habitual donors is important for several reasons. First, habitual donors account for more than 78 percent of the contributions made by members of the congressional donor pool who give contributions of $200 or more. Thus habitual donors are a primary source of campaign funds. They are therefore the most likely source of the representational distortion that results from the financing of congressional elections. Moreover, habitual donors are more routinely asked to give by candidates than are occasional donors, and they are more likely to have developed standing rules that help them decide whether to respond positively to a solicitation. One such rule is routinely contributing to the same set of candidates. In fact, there is some limited evidence that donors are extremely loyal. Twenty-four percent of the significant donors who had contributed in 1978 had given to a House member who remained in office through 1996. Forty-six percent of these individuals continued to support that same House member over the course of this 18-year interlude. These "perpetual donors" include individuals who still live in the candidate's district as well as some who do not. More than two-thirds of those who have been represented by the same member of Congress for the last 18 years contributed to that member 18 years later. Even more surprising is the fact that 45 percent of the 1978 donors who are now represented by someone else in Congress continue to help finance the campaign of a member who represented them almost two decades ago.

Habitual donors contribute to more candidates than do occasional donors. More than half of all occasional donors reported making a single contribution to a House or Senate candidate in 1996 (see table 2.2). Few gave to more than five candidates. In contrast, almost a quarter of habitual donors made only one contribution in 1996, and more than 60 percent say that they gave to between two and five candidates. Habitual donors clearly have a bigger footprint in the financing of congressional elections, but they do not fit the image of the stereotypical fat cat.

TABLE 2.2   THE NUMBER, SIZE, AND AMOUNT OF SIGNIFICANT DONORS' CONTRIBUTIONS TO CONGRESSIONAL CANDIDATES

	All	*Occasional*	*Habitual*
Number of candidates			
One	36%	52%	24%
Two to five	56	46	64
Six to ten	4	1	7
Eleven or more	4	1	6
Size of each contribution			
$200 or less	45%	45%	46%
$201 to $500	39	38	41
$501 to $999	16	11	19
$1000	29	20	37
Total amount contributed to House and Senate			
Less than $250	23%	31%	17%
$251 to $500	22	30	16
$501 to $1,000	26	23	28
$1,001 to $5,000	26	15	34
$5001 to $10,000	2	1	3
More than $10,001	1	1	1
(N)	(959)	(427)	(532)

Note: Chi-Square tests indicate that all differences between occasional and habitual donors are statistically significant at p<.001. Some columns do not add to 100 percent due to rounding. For the size of each contribution, columns do not add to 100 percent because some donors made contributions in each range.
Source: The Congressional Donors Survey.

The sizes of the contributions donors make also do not fit the fat-cat image. Occasional and habitual donors are equally likely to make small contributions of less than $200. They also are equally likely to make contributions of $200 to $500. However, habitual donors are considerably more likely to make contributions of larger amounts. This is particularly true of the major donors. Nearly three out of four made at least one contribution of $1,000.

Why would contributors who are quite willing to write checks for $1,000 also give much smaller amounts? The size of donors' contributions is to some degree a function of the amount requested. When contributors are invited to a dinner for $500 they often give that amount, but when they are invited to a barbeque with a suggested contribution of $100, they feel little impetus to give more. For this reason, professional fundraisers comb FEC records to determine how much a potential donor is likely to give.

We estimated the total amounts given by contributors from the number of contributions they claimed to have given within each range of amounts. Nearly one in three of all occasional donors gave $250 or less, usually a single contribution. More than 60 percent gave less than $500. Some habitual donors also gave small amounts; but more than 38 percent gave more than $1,000. While some donors clearly contribute significant sums to candidates, the typical donor is a relatively small player in the financing of congressional campaigns.

Checkbook Activists or Complete Activists?

Political contributors are sometimes criticized for being "checkbook citizens" whose only involvement in politics is giving money (but see Brown et al. 1980a; Hedges 1984). In fact, some scholars refer to contributions as "the junk food of participation, a relatively easy form of involvement that provides a certain number of empty participatory calories" (Verba et al. 1995, 518). For congressional donors, making a contribution to a political candidate or cause is probably easier than giving up personal time to volunteer in a political campaign. Congressional donors have the financial wherewithal to make a contribution. They also possess financial, policy, or personal motives to put money into the political arena. And, once they have made a contribution to a candidate, party, or PAC, they become the target of additional solicitations. As a result, individuals who enter the donor pool usually find themselves swimming in invitations to contribute.

The decision to work on a campaign involves another set of constraints. Making a contribution involves writing a check and perhaps attending a fundraising event with other donors. Working for a campaign requires a much larger time commitment, and it is easier for many donors to contribute money than time. A head of a corporation may work long hours for a seven- or eight-figure salary. Writing a check for $1,000 would have little impact on his financial circumstances, but spending five hours canvassing for a candidate in a shopping mall might consume a high portion of his free time. For many of these high-status businessmen and professionals, handing out leaflets at a shopping mall might seem to be a menial task of the sort that they hire people to perform in their personal and professional lives. As a consequence, few donors work regularly for political campaigns, and about half have never worked for a candidate for the House or Senate (see table 2.3). Similar percentages of donors have never worked for a presidential, state, or local candidate. Donors are even less likely to volunteer for party organizations and PACs. Indeed, more than 60 percent have never worked for a party committee and almost 80 percent have never worked for a PAC. Significant donors, like most political elites, lead full and busy lives, which discourages them from volunteering in political campaigns.

Habitual donors, however, are more likely than occasional donors to volunteer. More than 30 percent of habitual donors, for example, have worked in most elections for a House candidate, compared to just 4 percent of occasional donors. The numbers are similarly lopsided when comparing habitual and occasional donors who have worked in most elections for other candidates' campaigns, parties, or PACs. This suggests that many habitual donors are more than simply stereotypical checkbook activists.

There is one type of campaign activity that is common among all donors—soliciting campaign contributions. Nearly 60 percent of the congressional donors have asked someone else to give to a congressional candidate, and more than one-third have solicited contributions for a presidential candidate. Some of these solicitations may have been little more than asking a few friends along to a fundraising dinner. However, the large number of donors who solicit other people suggests that one of the important ways citizens enter the donor pool is by the invitation of friends, business associates, and neighbors. Moreover, it belies the narrow picture of checkbook citizens: these are individuals who create networks of social obligation. Someone may ask a neighbor to give to a community project,

TABLE 2.3. THE FREQUENCY OF VOLUNTEERING TO WORK ON A CAMPAIGN

	All	Occasional	Habitual
Worked for House candidates in:			
Most elections	19%	4%	31%
Some elections	34	39	30
Never	47	57	39
Worked for Senate candidates in:			
Most elections	14%	4%	23%
Some elections	32	32	32
Never	54	64	45
Worked for presidential candidates in:			
Most elections	16%	7%	22%
Some elections	30	29	30
Never	55	64	48
Worked for state or local candidates in:			
Most elections	21%	9%	30%
Some elections	37	44	31
Never	43	47	39
Worked for political party committees in:			
Most elections	14%	4%	21%
Some elections	26	27	24
Never	61	69	55
Worked for political action committees in:			
Most elections	7%	3%	10%
Some elections	15	11	19
Never	78	86	71
Worked for any type of candidate in most elections	29%	13%	43%
Worked for House or Senate candidate in most elections	21%	4%	34%
Worked for each type of candidate in most elections	8%	3%	14%
Never worked for candidates or committees	28%	35%	23%
Ever solicited money for:			
Congressional candidates	59%	46%	71%
Presidential candidates	35%	24%	46%
Political parties	29%	19%	39%
PACs	27%	21%	33%
(N)	(961)	(428)	(533)

Note: Chi-square tests indicate that all differences between occasional and habitual donors are statistically significant at p<.001. For the first six questions, some columns do not add up to 100 percent due to rounding. For the last two sets of questions the columns do not add up to 100 percent because some donors worked or solicited money for more than one type of candidate or political group.

Source: The Congressional Donors Survey.

and that neighbor may later ask her for a contribution on behalf of a political candidate (Brown et al. 1995). In the process of building donor and
social networks individuals engage in conversations about candidates
among themselves. These conversations usually occur in golf clubs, board
rooms, and other locations to which the average citizen has no access.

WHO GIVES?

If the donor pool looked like America, one might not care that a small
number of donors provide so much of the funding for congressional candidates. But the donor pool clearly looks like an "upper-class choir." Contributors to House and Senate campaigns are overwhelmingly rich and
well-educated, and they are also overwhelmingly middle-aged white men
(see table 2.4).

The fact that donors are much wealthier than other citizens should
come as no surprise. It takes money to give money. Although some mid-
dle-income families could afford a $1,000 campaign contribution, they
might prefer to spend the money on a new refrigerator, a home-entertain-
ment center, or a vacation. If nothing else, they would think long and hard
about giving the money to a candidate, weighing the opportunity costs of
a contribution against the many other things the money could buy. These
opportunity costs are far less relevant to the wealthiest Americans, who do
not have to defer consumption in order to make campaign contributions.

The magnitude of the income gap between average Americans and
campaign contributors is striking. Sixty-five percent of citizens reported
incomes of less than $50,000, but this includes only 4 percent of signifi-
cant donors. Only 8 percent of citizens had incomes of $100,000 or above,
but 78 percent of significant donors had incomes in this category. Fully 14
percent of significant donors had incomes of more than $500,000 per year.

The gap in education is almost as large. Nearly half of all citizens had
no more than a high-school education, whereas only 5 percent of significant donors fell into this category. Only 29 percent of citizens had a college degree, compared with 83 percent of significant donors. Nearly half
of significant donors have graduate or professional degrees.

These disparities in income and education are reflected in the occupations of donors and everyday citizens. Overall, businessmen and professionals dominate the donor pool. Nearly half of the donors are executives
from large or small businesses, and another 30 percent practice law or

TABLE 2.4. SIGNIFICANT DONORS' SOCIOECONOMIC STATUS

	All	Occasional	Habitual	Citizens
Education				
High school or less	5%	4%	5%	44%
Some college	13	17	10	27
College degree	23	25	21	19
Some graduate	11	9	13	NA
Graduate/professional degree	49	46	51	10
Income				
$50,000 or less	4%	5%	4%	65%
$50,000 to $99,999	17	19	15	27
$100,000 to $249,999	40	43	38	8
$250,000 to $500,000	24	20	27	0
More than $500,000	14	13	15	0
Occupation				
Large-business executive	36%	33%	39%	12%
Small-business executive	12	11	12	NA
Attorney	17	17	17	—
Medical professional	13	12	13	1
Education or media	11	14	8	2
Government/politics	6	6	7	—
Other/retired/NA	6	7	4	85
Job involves politics or government				
Elected office	5%	5%	5%	NA
Government staff	2	3	2	NA
Lobbyist	6	6	6	NA
Party official	2	2	1	NA
Consultant	1	1	1	NA
PAC official	1	1	1	NA
Other political job	5	4	6	
(N)	(946)	(421)	(525)	(1,714)

Note: The designation "—" indicates less than 0.5 percent. Chi-square tests indicate that differences between occasional and habitual donors are statistically significant at p<.01 for education and at p<.05 for income. The figures for citizens' occupation are from the 1990 census. Population figures do not distinguish between citizens as large or small business executives. The number reported for citizens as large business executives refers to those in the broader category of business occupations. Some columns do not add up to 100 percent due to rounding.
Source: The Congressional Donors Survey, the 1996 American National Election Study, and the Bureau of the Census.

medicine. A smaller number are employed in education, the media, and other occupations. Fully 22 percent of the significant donors hold jobs that involve politics or government, and a remarkable 24 percent of the major donors described themselves as lobbyists. It is likely that some donors contribute because they seek to be in a position to ask favors from powerful politicians, because their occupations put them in a position to be pressured for contributions by those same politicians, or for both reasons.

What is surprising about the socioeconomic status of donors is not its level but its uniformity. Virtually all of the donors have at least a college degree and earn $100,000 a year or more. Habitual donors are only slightly better educated and somewhat more affluent than occasional donors. The subset of habitual donors comprising major donors, on the other hand, have much larger incomes. Almost half of all major donors have incomes of more than $500,000 a year, and nearly all have incomes above $250,000.

The demographic characteristics of significant donors further show them to be an elite population. The overwhelming majority of donors are white (see table 2.5). African Americans constitute just one-half of one percent (0.5 percent) of all these individuals, a finding that is consistent with other studies of campaign contributors (Brown et al. 1995). Even African American candidates tend to rely on white donors. Jesse Jackson's 1996 presidential campaign might have sought to build a rainbow coalition, but that coalition-building process was funded by money raised primarily from white donors (Brown et al. 1995).

More than three out of four congressional donors are male. The "Year of the Woman" brought many new women members to Congress and women have overtaken men as a proportion of the voting population since 1992, but women clearly have a long way to go before they achieve equality in campaign contributing. Moreover, those women who give are more likely than men to be occasional donors, and they give smaller amounts to fewer candidates.

Donors are much older than the average American, and habitual donors are older than occasional donors. It takes time to amass the wealth and job security needed to become a significant donor, and even more time to become a permanent member of the donor pool. Almost no donors are less than 30 years of age, and 40 percent are over 60 years of age.

Individuals who are under age 45 have not yet reached their peak earning years, may have children at home or in college, and may be still

TABLE 2.5. SIGNIFICANT DONORS' DEMOGRAPHIC AND SOCIAL CHARACTERISTICS

	All	Occasional	Habitual	Citizens
Age				
18-30	1%	1%	1%	19%
31-45	17	22	12	39
46-60	42	43	42	20
61 or over	40	34	45	22
Sex				
Male	78%	73%	82%	48%
Female	22	28	18	52
Race				
White	95%	95%	95%	76%
African-American	1	1	1	12
Hispanic	1	2	1	9
Asian	1	2	–	2
Other	2	1	3	1
Region				
Northeast	24%	25%	24%	20%
Midwest	20	19	20	24
West	21	23	19	22
South	35	34	37	35
Religious tradition				
Evangelical Protestant	11%	14%	10%	27%
Mainline Protestant	41	33	47	23
Catholic	23	28	19	27
Jewish	12	12	11	2
Secular	8	8	8	12
Other	6	5	6	9
Frequency of attendance				
More than weekly	10%	10%	9%	12%
Weekly	26	27	26	14
Monthly	16	15	17	27
Few times a year	25	25	25	18
Seldom or never	23	23	24	29
(N)	(960)	(427)	(533)	(1,714)

Note: The designation "—" indicates less than 0.5 percent. Chi-square tests indicate that differences between occasional and habitual donors are statistically significant at p<.001 for age and sex. The figures for citizens' race are from the 1990 census. Some columns do not add up to 100 percent due to rounding.
Source: The Congressional Donors Survey; the 1996 American National Election Study; and the Bureau of the Census.

paying for their homes. They also may not have reached the point in their careers where others pressure them to give. In contrast, those who are over 60 have reached their earnings plateau, and the expenses for their homes and children may have decreased. The younger age of occasional donors supports the notion that some are habitual donors in the making.

Religion matters in many aspects of politics, including campaign finance. Although mainline Protestants are declining as a religious bloc as a result of the aging of their congregations, they still constitute a major force in financing elections. They comprise 41 percent of significant donors, although they are only 23 percent of the public. These denominations—Episcopalians, Methodists, Presbyterians, Lutherans, and Congregationalists, among others—once made up the upper strata of America's political elite (Wald 2003). Mainline Protestants also have long been involved in Republican Party politics (Layman 2001).

In contrast, evangelical Protestants, who now play a major role in Republican politics comprise only 11 percent of significant donors. These Baptist, Pentecostal, and nondenominational churches are the prime constituency of the Christian Right, and they constitute a major portion of Republican activists. Their low numbers among congressional donors reflect in part their lack of affluence. Evangelicals may have acquired the habit of voting in primaries and general elections and of working to influence party platforms, but they have yet to develop the habit of giving.

Catholics are the second-largest religious category among significant donors, and they are about as common among donors as they are in the population. Jews account for approximately 2 percent of the population but constitute 12 percent of all significant donors. Moreover, they account for nearly four out of ten major donors. American Jews have a long tradition of contributing to politics, cultural institutions, and charities. As a diaspora, they play close attention to national and international affairs. They have high levels of political activism, and deep concerns for the security of Israel, the protection of civil liberties, and other liberal causes. Their overrepresentation is a testimony to these traditions (Fuchs 1980).

Regardless of their religious tradition, significant donors are more likely than other Americans to attend church weekly or more often. This is especially the case for Catholics, of whom 45 percent attend church weekly and 13 percent attend church more than one time per week. In terms of their income, education, race, gender, age, as well as religion, significant donors are not typical of the U.S. population.

CONTINUITY AND CHANGE IN THE DONOR POOL

Congressional donors are part of a large and relatively stable pool of citizens who regularly spend money in politics. Yet change does occur: every election cycle some Americans make their first significant contribution to a congressional candidate, and others exit the donor pool because of declining interest in politics, a change in job, or death. In 1978 only 10 percent of all House donors reported making their first contribution to a House candidate, only 5 percent stated they had not previously contributed to a congressional or presidential candidate, and only 2 percent stated they had never previously contributed to a candidate in any type of election (Powell 1979).[3] There is no evidence to suggest that there were more new significant donors in 1996. The donor pool is relatively calm, with only a few new contributors trickling in during any particular election.

Of course, it is possible that the slow but steady influx of new contributors has gradually changed the composition of the donor pool. In 1976, the FECA sought to limit the impact of fat cats in financing campaigns and to encourage candidates to solicit contributions from a broader group of citizens. From 1976 to 1996, the maximum legal contribution remained constant but the costs of campaigns rapidly increased. This forced candidates to reach out to more potential donors in order to finance their campaigns, resulting in an increase in the size of the donor pool. For example, in 1978 the typical major-party general election candidate for the House raised almost $113,000. If that candidate chose to run again in 1996, he or she would have raised $458,000. If this candidate sought to finance his or her campaign with contributions averaging $200, he or she would need to raise contributions from 1,725 new donors.

Moreover, changes in society may have altered the social characteristics of donors. The period between 1978 and 1996 was marked by significant social change and a growing demographic diversity in Congress. African Americans increased their numbers markedly in the House, and Jesse Jackson ran twice for the presidency—often asking church congregations for money to help him get to his next campaign stop. During the 1990s, women increased their presence in the House and Senate and in many state legislatures. Women's PACs, such as EMILY's List, also built networks of women donors. Meanwhile, some more senior members of the donor pool, mostly white men, were exiting from it, largely as a result of their retirements and other changes in personal circumstances. These life-cycle effects may have had consequences for the representativeness of the donor pool.

Did candidates' needs or societal change alter the donor pool between 1978 and 1996? The answer is: not that much. Indeed, the lack of change is striking. Contributors in 1996 were somewhat better educated, somewhat wealthier, and somewhat older than in 1978—certainly not what changes in the law, campaigns, and society would predict. The portion of donors with graduate degrees increased somewhat from 34 percent to 49 percent. The numbers with incomes over $100,000 in 1978 was 37 percent: this figure would translate to about $230,000 in 1996 dollars, and 38 percent of significant contributors in 1996 had incomes of more than $250,000. The share of donors over 61 years of age increased from one-quarter to two-fifths over this 18-year period.

In addition, the donor pool is just as white, and possibly just as male, in 1996 as it was in 1978. African Americans have not moved into the donor pool, despite the growing number of African American professionals and the growing number of African Americans in Congress. It is possible that African Americans are growing in the ranks of donors of less than $200, although a recent survey of donors to presidential candidates in 2000 did not reveal many African American donors gave smaller amounts to either Gore or Bradley (Cooper et al. 2002).

In both 1978 and 1996, women constituted roughly 17 percent of all House donors. Yet there are reasons to suspect that women have increased their levels of giving. Women are more likely to contribute to Senate candidates, and 33 percent of all 1996 Senate donors were women. Women Senate candidates and EMILY's List have worked hard to build lists of female donors, and it seems likely this has resulted in an increase in women Senate donors. However, the lack of available evidence for women's contributions to 1978 Senate candidates limits us to speculation. Regardless, the donor pool is still biased toward very wealthy middle-aged white men.

The fact that the size of the donor pool has expanded significantly since 1978, but the social profile of significant donors has changed little, suggests that campaign fundraisers look for new donors among the friends, neighbors, and colleagues of current donors. As chapter 4 will show, many candidates ask their donors to seek out new contributors to help finance their campaigns, and donors are likely to turn to people who are very much like them.

Group Involvement

Congressional donors are embedded in a web of voluntary associations, as are most political elites. Membership in one group frequently leads to invitations to join others. Members of the Sierra Club are often invited to join the League of Conservation Voters, and members of the NRA are sometimes invited to join Gun Owners of America. Sometimes group memberships take on seemingly odd configurations, such as when members of the Sierra Club who own a hunting license are invited to join the NRA. Of course, business executives and professionals are often invited to join all types of groups.

Group members often become donors when they are solicited by candidates or interest-group leaders. For example, members of the Sierra Club routinely receive the magazine *Sierra*, which includes lists of candidates the organization endorses. Some organizations routinely rent their membership lists to sympathetic candidates and groups that employ these lists to solicit funds. The NRA and other conservative groups mobilize their members on behalf of conservative candidates, including encouraging them to make donations to congressional candidates. Group membership is a form of political activism that stimulates political participation and contributing (Rosenstone and Hansen 1993).

The typical significant donor belongs to five different types of groups, including professional-oriented groups, issue-specific groups, broad-based ideological groups, and civic or church-based associations. Contributors are more involved in civil society than the image of checkbook activists would imply. These networks of organizations to which they belong provide them with additional resources to influence public policy.

Nearly two-thirds of the donors are members of business or professional organizations, and nearly half are members of both types of these organizations (see table 2.6). More than 80 percent belong to a business group, a professional organization, or both. In contrast, only 2 percent of the donors are members of labor unions. However, these are not blue-collar unions. The unions they belong to primarily represent government employees, college professors, and other professionals rather than Teamsters and longshoremen. Clearly, these union members have a different life experience than members of the United Mine Workers of America or the Carpenters and Joiners Union.

In contrast, there is more diversity in the types of political advocacy groups to which the donors belong. Both liberal and conservative noneconomic groups are represented in the donor pool. Slightly more than one-quarter of all significant donors are members of environmental groups, and about one in seven belong to women's groups, civil rights

TABLE 2.6. SIGNIFICANT DONORS' AND CITIZENS' MEMBERSHIP IN GROUPS AND ORGANIZATIONS

	All	*Occasional*	*Habitual*	*Citizens*
Professional	64%	64%	63%	23%
Business	63	60	66	NA
Labor union	2	4	1	12
Political	NA	NA	NA	14%
Environment	27	22	32	NA
Women's	14	14	14	4
Pro-choice	17	15	19	NA
Civil rights	16	14	18	NA
Gun owner group	23	20	26	NA
Pro-family	12	11	12	NA
Pro-life	10	10	11	NA
Christian conservative	5	4	6	NA
Party	43	34	50	5
Ideological	31	23	38	1
Conservative	21	15	26	NA
Liberal	10	9	12	NA
Fraternal	18	14	20	8
Civic	50	42	57	3
Community	43	39	45	NA
Church	64	64	64	NA
(N)	(960)	(427)	(533)	(1,714)

Note: The designation "—" indicates less than 0.5 percent. Chi-square tests indicate that differences between occasional and habitual donors are statistically significant at p<.001 for environmental, party, conservative, and civic groups. Differences are statistically significant at p<.05 for business groups, labor unions, gun-owner groups, and fraternal organizations. The figures for citizens in professional organizations comprise a broader category that includes business organizations. The figures for citizens in party organizations also include candidate organizations. The figures for citizens in fraternal organizations include service organizations. Columns do not add up to 100 percent because donors often belonged to more than one organization.
Source: The Congressional Donors Survey and the 1996 American National Election Study.

groups, or pro-choice groups. Another one-fourth have memberships in gun ownership groups, and about one in ten belong to pro-life or pro-family groups.

Significant donors also are active in broad-based ideological organizations, such as the National Committee for an Effective Congress and the Freedom and Opportunity Society. Approximately one out of five donors are members of broad conservative groups, a figure far higher than that for broad liberal groups. This points to an important distinction between conservative and liberal donors. The former are far more likely to belong to general ideological groups, whereas liberal donors are more likely to be members of groups with more narrowly focused agendas. Finally, donors are involved in community and civic organizations and in their local churches. Church membership is as common as membership in a business or professional organization.

Do significant donors belong to groups that are aligned ideologically, or do some conservatives and liberals have memberships in the same associations? We created an index of membership in conservative organizations (pro-life, pro-gun, Christian conservative, conservative) and liberal groups (environmental, pro-choice, civil rights, and liberal).[4] Only 10 percent of the donors belonged to at least one conservative group and one liberal group. The most frequent combination was an environmental group and a pro-gun group (5 percent reported belonging to one of each), followed by a pro-gun group and a pro-choice group (2.5 percent reported belonging to one of each). Many of these individuals are from the Northwest, where liberal conservationists and conservative gun owners are in agreement about the need to protect the environment.

In sum, donors belong to a wide array of groups. Many belong to a narrow set of business and professional groups, but they are also involved in a wide variety of issues and ideological groups. Thus, although they do not speak with a unified political voice on social issues, the homogeneity of their economic-group memberships suggests they do indeed speak with an upper-class accent.

PARTISAN DIFFERENCES IN THE DONOR POOL

Many of the groups to which congressional donors belong have established strong ties to one political party or the other. Some groups that once sought to be bipartisan, such as environmental groups, gun control groups, and pro-choice and pro-life groups, now primarily support only one party. The contemporary Democratic Party includes a coalition of feminists, environmentalists, ethnic and racial minorities, and union members. The core of the Republican Party, by contrast, consists of business executives, gun enthusiasts, and religious and social conservatives. Indeed, diverse and sometimes polarized coalitions are a defining aspect of American political parties (Schlesinger 1985; Green and Guth 1988, 1991; Shafer and Claggett 1995; Green et al. 1999).

The donor pool has a significant pro-Republican tilt. About one-half of all donors identify with or lean toward the GOP, as opposed to one-third who identify or lean toward the Democrats (see table 2.7). This contrasts sharply with the loyalties of the general public, which are slightly more likely to identify with or have inclinations toward the Democratic Party than the GOP.

Habitual donors were more likely than occasional donors to identify themselves as Republicans, but most active givers—the major donors— were the most Democratic group. The Democratic advantage in major donors does not offset the Republican edge among habitual and occasional donors: the total contributions of all Republican contributors are significantly higher than those reported by all Democrats.

The two parties raise their money from slightly different sets of elites. Both parties' contributors are affluent, but Democratic donors are some-

TABLE 2.7. THE PARTISANSHIP OF DONORS AND CITIZENS

	All	*Occasional*	*Habitual*	*Citizens*
Strong Democrat	12%	9%	15%	19%
Democrat	9	12	7	20
Leans Democrat	10	10	10	14
Pure Independent	19	23	16	8
Leans Republican	19	21	17	12
Republican	14	15	13	16
Strong Republican	17	10	22	13
(N)	(954)	(426)	(528)	(1,714)

Note: Chi-Square tests indicate that differences between occasional and habitual donors are statistically significant at p<.001. Some columns do not add to 100 percent due to rounding.
Source: The Congressional Donors Survey and the 1996 American National Election Study.

TABLE 2.8. PARTISAN DIFFERENCES IN SIGNIFICANT DONORS'
SOCIAL CHARACTERISTICS

	Democrats	Republicans	Independents
Gender			
Male	69%	84%	75%
Female	31	16	25
Income			
$99,999 or less	29%	19%	15%
$100,000–$249,999	38	42	42
$250,000 or more	34	40	43
Education			
Less than college	12%	21%	19%
College degree	16	27	24
Graduate school	72	52	57
Occupation			
Law	29%	12%	16%
Education/Media	15	10	11
Government	13	2	4
Business	23	41	36
Small business/Sales	5	12	15
Other	15	24	18
Job involves politics	31%	17%	20%
Officeholder	7	4	4
Staff	5	1	2
Lobbyist	8	5	7
Other	11	7	7
Religion			
Mainline Protestant	31%	50%	31%
Evangelical	8	13	14
Catholic	22	26	14
Jewish	22	4	17
Other	7	3	9
Secular	11	4	14
(N)	(304)	(468)	(181)

Note: Partisan differences are significant at p<.001. Some columns do not add up to 100 percent due to rounding.
Source: The Congressional Donors Survey.

what less affluent than GOP donors (see table 2.8). However, Democratic contributors are much more likely than their Republican counterparts to have graduate school training. More Democratic donors are lawyers, educators, people employed in the media, or people holding down political jobs. These positions require advanced degrees, but they are less likely to generate the truly exceptional incomes of the business executives who constitute the core of GOP contributors.

The Democrats' donor pool has more women than the Republicans' does, but both parties draw their funds primarily from white and middle-aged donors. Half of all Republican donors are mainline Protestant denominations that have traditionally had more affluent members, but Republicans also draw a surprising number of Catholic contributors. Evangelical Protestants are underrepresented in both parties, but they are concentrated among Republican donors. In contrast, Jews comprise nearly a quarter of all significant Democratic donors.

Democratic and Republican donors belong to the same set of economic groups. Large majorities of both are members of business or professional groups, and even among Democratic contributors there are few union members (see table 2.9). Labor unions are an essential part of the Democratic coalition, but they constitute only 4 percent of the significant donors and they are outnumbered 12 to 1 by members of business associations.

Nevertheless, partisan donors belong to different issue groups. Democrats are far more likely than Republicans to belong to pro-choice, civil-rights, and women's groups, and to liberal organizations. Approximately half of all Democrats belong to an environmental group. Republicans are more likely to belong to pro-gun, pro-life, pro-family, and Christian-conservative groups. However, Republican members of the donor pool are less likely to belong to partisan-allied groups than are Democrats. For example, only 16 percent of Republican significant donors are members of pro-life groups, in contrast to 37 percent of Democratic donors who are members of pro-choice groups. To a large degree these differences reflect the organizational components of the parties' coalitions. Nevertheless, there is at least some overlap in group memberships. Fifteen percent of all Republican significant donors are members of environmental groups.

TABLE 2.9. PARTISAN DIFFERENCES IN SIGNIFICANT DONORS'
GROUP MEMBERSHIP

	Democrats	Republicans	Independents
Professional	65%	61%	67%
Business	47	72	69
Labor union	3	1	3
Environmental	50%	15%	21%
Women's	24	8	12
Pro-choice	37	7	11
Civil rights	36	6	10
Gun owner group	10%	29%	28%
Pro-family	7	16	10
Pro-life	3	16	8
Christian conservative	—	7	9
Party	52%	47%	17%
Conservative	2	36	17
Liberal	31	1	1
Fraternal	11%	23%	16%
Civic	50	53	44
Community	44	43	40
Church	55	71	60
(N)	(304)	(468)	(181)

Note: The designation "—" indicates less than 0.5 percent. Chi-square tests indicate that differences are statistically significant at $p<.001$ for all groups except professional groups, labor unions, and civic groups. Columns do not add up to 100 percent because donors often belonged to more than one organization.
Source: The Congressional Donors Survey.

SUMMARY

There is much truth to the traditional stereotype of campaign contributors as wealthy, white, middle-aged businessmen and professionals. Congressional contributors come from a narrow stratum of American society, and despite a sharp increase in the number of people who contribute to congressional campaigns, there is little evidence that the donor pool has become more diverse, except perhaps in regard to gender. There are few African Americans, union members, or even women—and only a handful of donors of modest financial means—among the financiers of congressional elections. In addition to their socioeconomic advantages, donors also are members of many political groups. Their political integration provides them with advantages in politics.

Members of Congress rarely just ask contributors for money, they socialize with them and return their telephone calls. As the costs of campaigns have escalated, members report that they spend more time than ever contacting donors and asking for contributions. When members of Congress wander among the tables at fundraising events, they do not hear the voices of average Americans. Significant donors do not live paycheck to paycheck, or worry about where they will get the money for car repairs or for their children's educations. They do not need to buy television sets on credit, or think about their budget when considering whether to have dinner in a restaurant on Saturday night. This is true of Democratic and Republican donors alike, despite differences in the social characteristics of partisan donors.

Nevertheless, the advocacy groups to which the donors belong represent a range of ideological causes. Although the donor pool is relatively homogeneous in its social composition, the nature of the groups contained within it hints that donors may have different political views and different motives for participating in politics. That means that Democratic members of Congress and congressional candidates are likely to hear from members of business associations and liberal social/cultural groups and Republicans are likely to hear from the business sector and conservative social elites.

chapter 3

What Motivates Donors?

Most significant donors are drawn from a narrow slice of American society: they are primarily wealthy, white, male, business executives who are middle-aged or older. Does this mean that their political views and reasons for contributing are likely to advance the interests of this elite? Many citizens assume that individual businessmen give in pursuit of particularistic politics designed to benefit their businesses or industries at the expense of the general public. Most reform groups assume that all donors from a single firm coordinate their contributions to advance their mutual material interests.

Nevertheless, understanding the donor pool probably involves more than economics and demographic characteristics. Contributing to congressional candidates is an uncommon behavior even among the most affluent Americans. Even wealthy Americans can imagine other things to do with their money than to give it to congressional candidates. What motivates donors to give? Do they contribute mainly to advance their material interests, to forward certain issues or broad-based causes, for social reasons, or for a variety of seemingly random unclassifiable motives? Are their reasons for contributing and their viewpoints sufficiently diverse to undercut the political bias suggested by their demographic characteristics?

In this chapter, we explore the donors' reasons for contributing to congressional candidates. Then, we examine the connections between donors' motives and their background characteristics, frequency of giving, group membership, and ideological and issue positions. This enables us to determine whether they are, indeed, a homogeneous, materially self-interested group, or whether they possess a diversity of motives and represent a variety of political views.

DONOR MOTIVES

Most people believe that donors make political contributions for financial reasons. Journalists who describe accounts generally assume that contributions are primarily motivated by economic policy goals. News stories regale readers and television viewers with the occupations of contributors in attendance at fundraising events, linking the donors' contributions to upcoming votes in congressional committees and on the House and Senate floors. Pollsters report that much of the public think of contributions that donors give to candidates as "bribery" (Morin and Brossard 1997). Political scientists' and historians' accounts of campaign contributions focus almost exclusively on giving by businessmen, detailing examples of donors who admitted they gave contributions in order to secure government contracts and leases or to escape regulations and taxes (Overacker 1932).

Yet, all political participation is not motivated by "material" incentives. Some political activism, including campaign contributions, is motivated by what are referred to as "purposive" and "solidary" goals (Clark and Wilson 1961; Wilson 1973; Brown et al. 1980a, 1980b; Brown, Powell, and Wilcox 1995; Verba et al. 1995). Purposive or ideological motives are mostly concerned with enacting general public policies or providing public goods that apply equally to large classes of society. Solidary or social motives involve the psychological benefits that stem from the social side of political participation.

Donors with material motives seek tangible personal gain from their contributions. These "investors" typically desire broad policies to benefit their industry, narrow policies to benefit their company, or even narrower policies to benefit themselves. Investors often view a contribution as part of a larger government relations strategy. They give contributions to make it easier for a lobbyist to get the attention of a member of Congress the first time, to thank a member for supporting a specific piece of legislation, or to help maintain an ongoing relationship that affords company or industry lobbyists continued political access (see, e.g., Biersack, Herrnson, and Wilcox 1994, 1999). Some investors contribute with little prodding.

They recognize that making a donation to the legislators and candidates they routinely contact is necessary for them to do their job effectively. They consider contributions similar to the dues they pay various professional associations and social clubs–something one needs to "pay in order to play."

Others contribute in response to solicitations from business associates. Peer pressure and competition for promotions can motivate members of a firm to make a contribution of $200 or more. Business executives may feel obligated to respond to solicitations from colleagues outside their firms with whom they often cooperate in lobbying efforts. Tom Smith, who we described in chapter 1, is an example of an investor. He contributed to congressional candidates, mainly incumbents, in order to ensure he had the access he needed to make arguments on behalf of the insurance industry.

Donors with purposive motives contribute in order to advance their positions on salient issues, such as abortion rights, gun ownership, or environmental protections, or to advance some vision of the good society, whether one regulated by a free market, involving government programs to help the disadvantaged, or some other governing philosophy. These "ideologues" support candidates who share their issue positions and philosophies. They are more likely to contribute in competitive races, where their contributions and those of others like them have the potential to influence an election outcome. In the first chapter, we described Harriet White, an ideologue, who contributed primarily to help elect candidates who supported tougher environmental laws.

Contributors with solidary motives enjoy the social aspects of giving—friendship, social events, and recognition. These "intimates" give because they are friends with the candidate or the person who asked them to make the contribution. Other intimates contribute because the solicitation involves a fundraising event that gives them the opportunity to socialize with influential politicians, movie stars and other celebrities, and individuals like themselves. Many intimates enjoy the public recognition they receive from making a large contribution. Dick Jones (the hypothetical broadcaster discussed in chapter 1), who routinely contributes to a politician who is a longtime friend, and who visits with many other friends at the candidate's fundraising events, is an example of an intimate. Of course, many donors have a mix of these motives. Charles Kushner (also discussed in chapter 1), is an example of a congressional donor who gives for material, purposive, and social concerns.

MEASURING MOTIVES

To learn why significant donors contribute to candidates, we asked them to specify the importance of each of several broad-based reasons for making a donation and to identify some specific factors that influenced their decisions to contribute to specific candidates. Large majorities of contributors indicated that influencing elections is always important to them. Seventy-three percent reported it was very important to support a candidate or cause, and another 23 percent stated it is somewhat important (see table 3.1). Only 4 percent stated this is not very important. More than 60 percent maintained that influencing an election outcome or public policies is very important, and roughly 30 percent stated these factors are somewhat important. Few donors indicated that material or solidary goals were very important, although larger numbers said that these factors were somewhat important.

Donors most often cited policy-related factors or personal connections when asked about the factors that motivate them to make individual contributions. These include ideology, an unacceptable opponent, candidates' issue positions, partisanship, a personal relationship with a candidate, being asked by someone they knew, or supporting a local politician. Business-related reasons were acknowledged much less often, although a combined 60 percent admitted that it was always or sometimes important whether a candidate was friendly to their industry, and more than half said that it was at least sometimes important to give so that their business was treated fairly. Only 26 percent indicated that they always or sometimes consider the opportunity to attend an event when deciding whether to make a contribution.

That purposive goals are a major factor in the decision to contribute is not surprising. Purposive motives influence donations to presidential candidates (Brown et al. 1980a, 1980b; Brown et al. 1995), political parties, PACs (Green and Guth 1986), and other political organizations (Baumgartner and Leech 1998). Indeed, the importance of purposive motives may have increased in recent years, as the parties have diverged in their policy stances and party margins in Congress have narrowed, making the outcome of a handful of races critically important to those who care about the policies on which the parties differ.

Yet, there are reasons to believe that these data overemphasize purposive motives. First, it is socially less acceptable to say that you give for

TABLE 3.1 SIGNIFICANT DONORS' REASONS FOR MAKING A CONTRIBUTION TO A CONGRESSIONAL CANDIDATE

	Very Important	Somewhat Important	Not Very Important
To support a candidate or cause	73%	23	4
To make a difference in the outcome of an election	61%	30	9
To influence policies of government	61%	29	10
For business or employment reasons	8%	28	64
It is expected of someone in my position	4%	19	78
Enjoyment of friendship and social contacts	3%	20	78
It gives me a feeling of recognition	1%	14	85
(N)			(1,027)

	Always Important	Sometimes Important	Seldom Important
Candidate's liberalism-conservatism	69%	24	7
Candidate is from my district or state	66%	24	11
Candidate's opponent is unacceptable	49%	43	8
I know the candidate personally	47%	32	20
Candidate's position on a specific issue	35%	41	24
Candidate's party	31%	38	32
Candidate is in a close race	25%	51	24
Asked by someone I know personally	25%	49	27
Candidate friendly to industry or work	25%	35	40
So my business will be treated fairly	23%	28	49
A group I respect supports the candidate	12%	47	40
Asked by someone I don't want to say no to	9%	27	63
Candidate's seniority, committee, or leadership position	8%	43	50
Candidate is likely to win the election	7%	37	56
Involves an event I want to attend	4%	22	74
People in my line of work are giving	4%	22	74
(N)			(1,018)

Note: Some rows do not add up to 100 percent due to rounding.
Source: The Congressional Donors Survey.

business reasons than that you give to support a candidate, even if the candidate's pro-business stance is the donor's sole reason for supporting a candidate. It is also less acceptable to state that you contribute because you want to attend an event than to say that you gave because the person from whom you received an invitation is a friend. Moreover, of the three sets of incentives, only purpose motives fit a popular normative conception for making campaign contributions—namely, that the donor supports the candidate's issue positions.

Second, for many donors there is a blending of material, purposive, and solidary goals. Thus donors who seek narrow policy benefits for their business may state they contribute to influence government policy, to support a candidate or a cause, or because of a candidate's position on specific issues. Long-term investors may direct their contributions to incumbents with a pro-business ideology in order to gain access or to candidates in close races in an attempt to build a pro-business Congress (Ferguson 1995). Indeed, in recent years the business community has succeeded in channeling large sums of individual contributions to candidates in specially targeted races where pro-business candidates face opponents who are supportive of labor or environmental regulations (Nelson and Biersack 1999).

To explore these underlying motives, we derived a three-factor solution that is consistent with previous research. The results confirm that donors contribute in pursuit of material, purposive, and solidary goals. However, there are some subtle distinctions among ideologues. One group of ideologues indicated that they gave primarily to influence the outcome of elections and influence public policy. A second group indicated that their contribution decisions were influenced by advocacy group endorsements and the candidates' positions on specific issues. These donors tended to be members of environmental, civil-rights, or pro-choice groups. A third group of ideologues relied more on broad ideology or party affiliation when making their contribution decisions.

There also are some subtle differences among intimates. One group was heavily influenced by personal relationships. They stated that friendship with a candidate or a solicitor was always important in helping them to decide whether to contribute, or that there were some solicitors whom they felt they could not refuse. A second group of intimates were locally oriented in their contributing activity. They indicated that community ties were always important in their decision-making. They always considered whether they knew the candidate personally or the candidate resided in

TABLE 3.2. FACTOR LOADINGS FOR SIGNIFICANT DONORS' MOTIVES FOR
CONTRIBUTING TO CONGRESSIONAL CANDIDATES

	Material items	*Purposive items*	*Solidary items*
Candidate's liberalism-conservatism	.019	.464	-.107
So business will be treated fairly	.821	.073	.087
Candidate is friendly to my industry			
tor work	.819	.035	.129
Involves an event I want to attend	.132	.001	.612
People in my line of work are giving	.570	-.210	.269
To influence the policies of government	.053	.652	.034
It is expected of someone in my position	.358	-.206	.476
For business or employment reasons	.766	-.093	.163
Enjoyment of the friendship and			
social contacts	.084	-.053	.754
To make a difference in the outcome of			
an election	-.101	.766	-.078
It gives me a feeling of recognition	.139	-.065	.748
To support a candidate or cause	-.155	.748	-.045
(N)			(981)

Note: The above factors are based on principal component solutions using oblique rotations.
Source: The Congressional Donors Survey.

their district or state when making a contribution. Finally, a third group indicated that they gave primarily because they enjoyed socializing at fundraising events.

The existence of these distinct sets of ideologues and intimates attests to the subtlety of donor motives, but in most important respects, the three sets of ideologues behave similarly, as do the three sets of intimates.[1] We created scales to measure the three motives associated with investors, ideologues, and intimates, but where there are meaningful differences among the ideologues or the intimates we discuss them (see table 3.2).

INVESTORS, IDEOLOGUES, AND INTIMATES

Many significant donors have more than one reason for contributing. One-fourth of all donors—the investors—are most strongly motivated by material incentives. The ideologues, comprising more than one-third of the donor pool, give for purposive reasons. Intimates, who make up one-quarter of the donors, give primarily for social reasons. Roughly 15 percent of the donors are labeled "incidentals." Despite the fact that they make contributions, they do not have strong motives to do so.

Investors

Large majorities of investors state that they always consider whether a candidate is friendly to their business or industry and has treated their business fairly prior to making a contribution (see table 3.3). Indeed, 63 percent of investors report that it is always important that a candidate treat their business fairly; another 22 percent state that it is at least sometimes important. Similar numbers of investors point to business reasons as im-

TABLE 3.3. INVESTORS', IDEOLOGUES', INTIMATES', AND INCIDENTALS' REASONS FOR MAKING A CONTRIBUTION TO A CONGRESSIONAL CANDIDATE

	Investors	Ideologues	Intimates	Incidentals
Candidate is friendly to my industry or work	63%	10%	21%	4%
So my business will be treated fairly	58	10	20	1
For business or employment reasons	28	—	5	—
People in my line of work are giving	10	—	6	—
To support a candidate or cause	60	98	66	46
To make a difference in the outcome of an election	50	93	48	27
Candidate's liberalism-conservatism	62	88	60	55
To influence the policies of government	52	88	56	25
Involves an event I want to attend	2	2	12	—
It is expected of someone in my position	7	—	7	—
Enjoyment of friendship and social contacts	—	—	10	—
It gives me a feeling of recognition	—	—	3	—
(N)	(247)	(356)	(236)	(143)

Note: The designation "—" indicates less than 0.5 percent. Chi-square tests indicate that all differences between donors are statistically significant at $p<.001$. Figures represent the percentages of donors who report that each reason is always or very important. Columns do not add up to 100 percent because donors often cited more than one reason for making a contribution.
Source: The Congressional Donors Survey.

portant to their contributions. In contrast, more than 70 percent of ideologues, intimates, and incidentals state that business considerations are never important to their contribution decisions.

Many investors state that contributions are important for them to gain access to House and Senate incumbents to assure that their economic interests are protected. As one investor explained:

> I give modestly to gain access to the political process. My business is heavily regulated and it is important that we be treated fairly, both my firm and my industry. Most people have no idea how hard it is to get bureaucrats and legislators to pay attention, and being part of the process helps. Money helps on the administrative end. Take national health insurance. I think most of these proposals are counterproductive, so I'm against them. But something might pass, and I need to be involved in the implementation of the policy.

Not surprisingly, some also cite taxes and appropriations as important concerns. A majority of the investors are Republican and identify themselves as some type of conservative.

Ideologues

Ideologues are virtually unanimous in stating they make contributions in order to support a specific candidate or cause, and 93 percent maintain that affecting election outcomes or helping to support a candidate or cause is very important. Almost nine out of ten of these donors state that they consider a candidate's place on the political spectrum always important and that the candidates' willingness to pursue certain policies is very important in their contribution decisions. Investors and intimates also state that these factors are important, although they report this significantly less often than do ideologues.

Ideologues care deeply about specific issues, broader political philosophy, and partisan control of Congress. As one ideologue made clear:

> I make campaign contributions for one reason and one reason only: to influence the philosophy of government. I look for candidates who share my perspective. If a politician won't come clean on his basic philosophy, then no money from me. I respect

people with strong values, even if I think their values are wrong. I don't like "go along, get along" politicians.

Unlike investors, ideologues tend to discuss public issues that are unrelated to their material well-being. As one ideologue explained:

> I give politically because I want to try to influence the public policy decisions that are made and I want to help try to get elected who I think will make the right decisions on various matters of public policy. . . . I have never given one penny to advance any personal economic interest of mine or the economic interest of a client or anybody else.

One summarized the importance that she places on social issues:

> Somebody who would be strictly anti-abortion across the board really troubles me. Another big issue would be affirmative action. I'm troubled by our scaling back of affirmative action programs. Anybody who would say that they were against all affirmative action programs, I would be very much against.

Another ideologue emphasized environmental policy:

> To me the bottom line is environmental policy: if we don't stop despoiling the air and the water, there will be no political system to worry about in the future. So, I have a kind of test for candidates, namely, where do they stand on the environment? Now, this is a fairly complicated thing because there are lots of environmental issues. My evaluation is sort of a sum of the issues I care about.

The "electoral connection" is very important to most ideologues. They seek to contribute their money in close contests in order to maximize the number of legislators who support their political positions. This strategy gives these donors the best opportunity to get the biggest bang for their buck in terms of influencing individual elections. It also enables them to influence the overall composition of Congress. By electing new members or helping to reelect endangered incumbents they help influence the partisan control of Congress, enhance the prospects of their pet issues getting a favorable hearing in the legislative process, or increase the possibility that the governmental process will move the nation in the direction of their political philosophy. As one contributor stated:

> I give money to those who share my views. There also has to be a need. If they don't have a worthy opponent then they don't need my money. They have to share my views and be willing to help with my interests. I define these things pretty broadly. I don't expect any quid pro quo. I just support people who believe in the free enterprise system and limited government.

Intimates

Intimates are more likely than any other congressional donors to place a heavy emphasis on being invited to a fundraising event, having the opportunity to socialize, or obtaining some sort of recognition in return for their contribution. For example, 72 percent of all intimates maintain that friendship and social contact are at least somewhat important in their contributing, as opposed to 11 percent of the investors and 7 percent of the ideologues.

Some intimates explained they made contributions because they enjoyed contact with candidates. For some, political motives do not enter into the decision to make a contribution at all; they give solely because they were asked by a close friend. Other intimates wanted to rub elbows with influential members of Congress and other elites, including the movie stars and athletes that are occasionally the headliners for fundraising events. Some enjoy working with others to pursue a political goal in a social setting. As an engineer and self-described "people person" explained:

> I really enjoy politics. I like to write checks, lick stamps, shake hands, and argue about issues. . . . I am most influenced by friends and I influence them as well. . . . I really do it all: I write [members of Congress], I talk, I testify, and I meet these guys socially.

Other intimates desire more than personal contact; they require a personal relationship with the candidate. One intimate donor explained, "I must know the candidate personally or I will not give money." Other intimates find group connections to be very important. As one emphasized:

Political finance happens through local groups: business groups, old boys' clubs, labor unions, churches, women's groups, and so forth. I belong to many different kinds of groups on the left and that is where we raise the money. . . . I do lots of volunteer work and give lots of money to charity, and campaign donations are just another side of this effort.

Intimates, in sum, contribute because they enjoy socializing with other political elites, or because of their ties to candidates and solicitors. In addition, many intimates desire to be recognized as influential members of their communities. Nevertheless, personalities are not everything to some of these donors. Many indicated that they only enjoy interacting with and contributing to those who share their basic political philosophy.

Incidentals

Incidentals make contributions for a variety of reasons, but the factors discussed above are less important to them than they are to investors, ideologues, and intimates. Moreover, the incidentals apply these factors with less consistency than do the other donors. Indeed, incidentals differ from the other donors in that they do not develop a set of consistent, recognizable, decision rules. They make fewer contributions.

SOCIAL AND POLITICAL SOURCES OF MOTIVES

Donor motives are not randomly distributed among congressional contributors. They are systematically related to income, gender, age, religion, partisanship, and group membership. The most affluent donors place the greatest emphasis on pursuing material goals, and these incentives increase along with donor incomes (see figure 3.1). Those with lower incomes are not economically prepared to pursue or obtain the same types of material benefits available to corporate executives and business leaders. Many wealthy donors also possess strong solidary incentives, and these, too, increase with donor incomes. Less affluent donors typically have purposive motives. They give primarily because they are inspired by controversial issues and causes. Moreover, they are less likely to benefit financially from

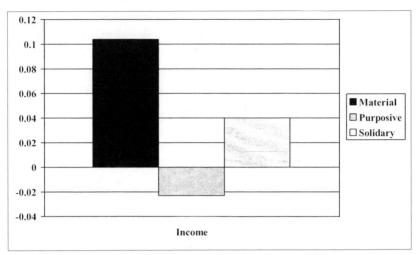

FIGURE 3.1 THE RELATIONSHIP BETWEEN DONOR MOTIVES AND INCOME

Note: The Figures are based on Kendall's Tau correlations. Income is an ordinal variable with five categories (1 = less than $50,000; 2 = $50,000 to $99,999; 3 = $1000,000 to 249,000; 4 = $250,000 to $500,000; 5 = above $500,000).
Source: The Congressional Donors Survey.

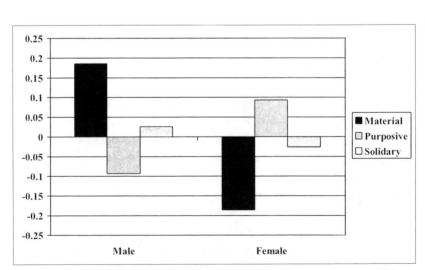

FIGURE 3.2 THE RELATIONSHIP BETWEEN DONOR MOTIVES AND GENDER

Note: The figures are based on Pearson's correlations.
Source: The Congressional Donors Survey.

contributions, or to be invited to the events that provide the greatest social benefits.

There is a gender gap in contributor motives. Compared to men, women are much less motivated by material benefits, and much more drawn to giving for purposive goals (see figure 3.2). There are fewer women in the upper levels of the business world, so fewer women are investors seeking to protect business interests. Rather, most women donors are ideologues who care about issues, such as abortion rights, environmental protections, social welfare issues, and breaking the glass ceiling in politics. Among congressional donors, liberal Democratic women outnumber their conservative Republican counterparts by a wide margin, although this is not true among presidential donors (Brown et al. 1995).

It is often said that young people are inspired by ideas and older people are inspired by money. Nevertheless, the youngest contributors, between thirty and forty-five years of age, are the most likely to pursue material motives. They are drawn into contributing by their business and professional networks (see figure 3.3). The oldest donors, who are typically retired, lose many of their reasons for pursuing their professional interests and face fewer compelling requests from their former colleagues. Younger donors also have more social motives for giving, presumably because they are more interested in making strong impressions and establishing social connections.

In contrast, younger donors are less concerned with issues and ideology than are middle-aged and elderly donors. Senior citizens, on the other hand, are the most strongly motivated by purposive goals. Ideology appears to be the only factor that sustains contributing after retirement. It is possible that most investors and many intimates drop out of the donor pool when they retire. It is also possible that motives change over the course of donors' lives and that they become more ideologically motivated as time goes on. The evidence garnered from individuals who were in the donor pool in 1978 and resurveyed in 1996 demonstrates that both of these processes are at work.

Members of different religious groups have different motives for contributing to congressional candidates (see figure 3.4). Mainline Protestants are especially interested in pursuing material motives. Wealthy business executives are often drawn into joining these high-status churches, where they frequently interact with other materially oriented donors. Evangelical Protestants, relative newcomers to political giving, are significantly less

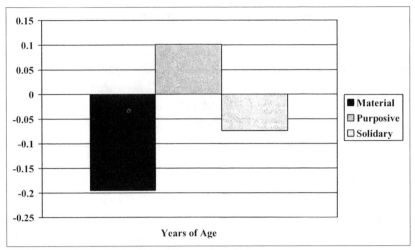

FIGURE 3.3 THE RELATIONSHIP BETWEEN DONOR MOTIVES AND AGE

Note: The figures are based on Pearson's correlations. "Years of age" is a continuous variable that reflects the donor's age as of 1996.

Source: The Congressional Donors Survey.

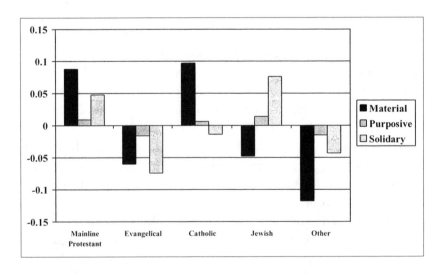

FIGURE 3.4 THE RELATIONSHIP BETWEEN DONOR MOTIVES AND RELIGION

Note: The figures are based on Pearson's correlations.

Source: The Congressional Donors Survey.

concerned with material gains and less interested in social benefits than other donors. It is somewhat surprising that Catholics are strongly motivated by material goals. There is a large contingent of Catholic Republican businessmen in the donor pool–indeed, in contrast to the general public, more than 60 percent of Catholic donors are Republicans. Jews, on the other hand, are more motivated by solidary and purposive concerns. Jews are not distinctively drawn to fundraising events, but they are more likely than other donors to be embedded in networks of friendship that motivate them to contribute (Levick-Segnatelli 1994; Brown et al. 1995).

People join different types of groups for different reasons, which are reflected in their motives for making campaign contributions. Not surprisingly, members of business groups such as the Chamber of Commerce and, to a lesser extent, professional groups such as the American Medical Association, have very strong material motives and very weak purposive motives (see figure 3.5). In contrast, members of liberal groups, including those concerned with the environment, a woman's right to choose, and civil rights, are strongly motivated by purposive goals and do not give in pursuit of personal profit. Members of conservative organizations have a variety of motives for contributing. Members of pro-life groups are influenced by purposive and material incentives. Members of Christian Conservative groups are motivated by purposive goals, but not by material gain. Somewhat surprisingly, members of pro-gun groups are strongly motivated by material concerns but not purposive goals. More than 90 percent of members of pro-gun groups are also members of business or professional organizations. Those pro-gun group members who are not involved in business networks are strongly motivated by purposive rather than material goals.

Partisanship has an important but somewhat complicated relationship with donor motives. In general, Democrats are less motivated by purposive concerns and especially material concerns, and are more attracted to the social benefits of giving (see figure 3.6). However, independent donors who lean toward the GOP—roughly one third of whom routinely contact members of Congress as part of their jobs—are far more motivated by material concerns. These donors have a professional incentive to call themselves independents in order to be able to lobby members of both parties, but their affluence and social location incline them toward the Republican Party. Partisans, especially strong Democrats, are more likely to value the social connections with politicians and other donors. Strong partisans of

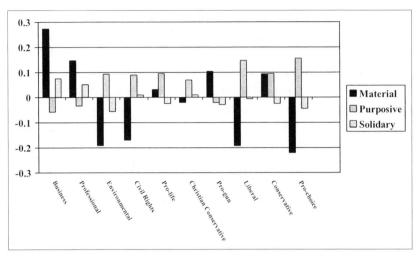

FIGURE 3.5 THE RELATIONSHIP BETWEEN DONOR MOTIVES AND
GROUP MEMBERSHIP

Note: The figures are based on Pearson's correlations. Membership in a political organization is a dummy measure (1 = member; 0 = not a member).
Source: The Congressional Donors Survey.

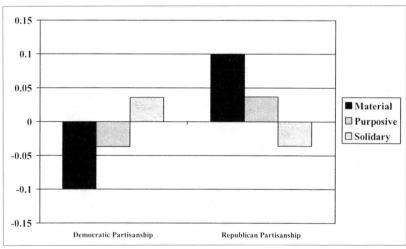

FIGURE 3.6 THE RELATIONSHIP BETWEEN DONOR MOTIVES AND
PARTY IDENTIFICATION

Note: The figures are based on Kendall's Tau correlations. Party identification is based on a seven-point scale in which 1 = Strong Republican; 4 = Independent; 7 = Strong Democrat.
Source: The Congressional Donors Survey.

both parties, who hold the most ideologically extreme political views, are the most likely to pursue purposive goals.

MOTIVES, CONTRIBUTING, AND POLITICAL VOLUNTEERISM

The congressional donors all have the financial wherewithal and motivation to give at least one $200 contribution to a congressional candidate. Nevertheless, some contribute to other types of candidates and others volunteer to work on political campaigns. Those who are motivated by purposive goals are the most likely to be habitual donors (see figure 3.7). Ideologues are the most likely to "go the extra mile" in giving, writing checks to many candidates, mainly in close elections across the country where they believe their money will have its biggest impact and perhaps influence the outcome of an election.

Motives also influence congressional donors' contributions to candidates who run for offices other than Congress. Investors—who are strongly

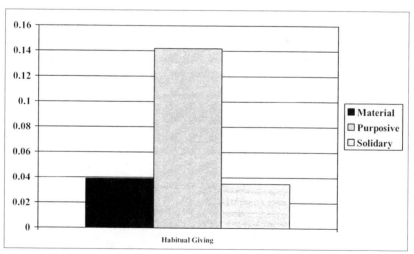

FIGURE 3.7 THE RELATIONSHIP BETWEEN DONOR MOTIVES AND HABITUAL GIVING

Note: The figures are based on Pearson's correlations. Habitual giving is a dummy measure defined as those who contribute to House or Senate candidates in most elections.
Source: The Congressional Donors Survey.

motivated by material concerns—more routinely contribute to House candidates, but not to candidates for the presidency or Senate. Ideologues are more likely to contribute to presidential and Senate candidates than to candidates for the House. Intimates are more likely to give to presidential and Senate candidates. These campaigns involve many more personal solicitation networks, sponsor flashier events, and offer more of the levels of formal recognition that intimates appreciate.

Contributions are not the only campaign activities related to donor motives. Intimates are especially likely to go beyond giving and to volunteer for House and especially Senate and presidential campaigns. They clearly see political campaigning as an opportunity for social interaction. Ideologues also volunteer on a variety of federal campaigns. Only investors do not devote much time to assisting those they would like to see in public office get elected. Rather than invest their time, they prefer to contribute their money.

POLITICAL ATTITUDES

The diversity in congressional donors' motives is mirrored in their political attitudes. Democratic donors and Republican donors have sharply different views about specific policies. They also have extremely different opinions of different social and political groups. Most donors are conservative on economic, social-welfare, and foreign-policy and defense issues, but moderate to liberal on social issues, but there are deep partisan divisions among them (see table 3.4). A majority of all donors favored tax cuts, even if they would lead to reduced spending, and a plurality opposed additional environmental safeguards.

Nevertheless, partisan donors are sharply divided on these issues. More than 80 percent of all Democratic donors oppose tax cuts and 78 percent favor environmental protections. Most Republicans take opposing positions on these issues: 75 percent support tax cuts and almost two-thirds oppose greater environmental protections. Independents are generally conservative on these issues, but not as conservative as the Republicans. Although only a small minority of donors favor a return to the gold standard (a perennial favorite issue of the Christian Right), a majority of Republicans are either neutral or supportive of the gold standard.

TABLE 3.4 THE INFLUENCE OF PARTISANSHIP ON SIGNIFICANT DONORS'
POLITICAL ATTITUDES

	All	*Democrats*	*Republicans*	*Independents*
Economic Issues				
Tax cuts even if it means reducing government services				
Conservative	51%	8%	75%	56%
Neutral	12	10	12	15
Liberal	37	82	13	29
More environmental protection even if higher prices/fewer jobs				
Conservative	45%	7%	65%	50%
Neutral	16	15	16	19
Liberal	39	78	19	31
Return to the gold standard				
Conservative	10%	3%	19%	20%
Neutral	35	30	38	34
Liberal	55	67	43	46
Social Welfare Issues				
More spending to reduce poverty and hunger				
Conservative	45%	9%	64%	48%
Neutral	18	14	20	19
Liberal	38	77	16	32
U.S. needs national health insurance				
Conservative	49%	11%	72%	45%
Neutral	14	14	11	23
Liberal	37	76	16	33
Foreign and Defense Policy				
Sharply reduce defense spending				
Conservative	55%	25%	72%	57%
Neutral	19	26	14	21
Liberal	26	49	14	22
Free trade even if loss of jobs				
Conservative	52%	45%	57%	50%
Neutral	22	27	19	24
Liberal	26	28	24	27

(continued on next page)

	All	Democrats	Republicans	Independents
Social and Cultural Issues				
Ban abortion except to save mother's life				
Conservative	27%	8%	40%	22%
Neutral	10	6	15	6
Liberal	63	86	46	72
Allow gays to teach in schools				
Conservative	33%	10%	46%	34%
Neutral	19	14	21	23
Liberal	48	76	33	44
Women have equal role in business, industry, and government				
Conservative	7%	1%	10%	7%
Neutral	10	4	12	15
Liberal	83	95	78	78
Country has gone too far in helping minorities				
Conservative	39%	9%	54%	45%
Neutral	22	13	27	20
Liberal	39	78	18	35
(N)	(1,040)	(314)	(202)	(524)

Note: Chi-square tests indicate that all differences between donors are statistically significant at p<.001. Some columns do not add up to 100 percent due to rounding.
Source: The Congressional Donors Survey.

Large majorities of Republican donors, like most Republican voters, also oppose additional spending to reduce poverty and hunger or to fund national health insurance. Not surprisingly, most Democratic donors hold opposing points of view, as do their core electoral constituencies (Erikson and Tedin 2000). Independents are more divided over social-welfare policies, but they are more conservative than liberal. The partisan divide also is evident on defense spending, but only a plurality of Democratic donors favor sharply reduced spending.

Trade issues cut across party lines. A plurality of Democrats joined a majority of Republicans and independents in support of free trade, even if it meant a loss of American jobs. They are opposed by roughly one-fourth of all Republican, Democratic, and independent donors. Business executives of both parties joined forces in support of free trade, while significant ideological constituencies of both parties, including labor and environmentalists for the Democrats and Christian Conservatives and isolationists for Republicans, oppose it. The politics of the North American Free Trade Act (NAFTA) exemplify the absence of partisan divisions on this issue, where every living president—Democrat and Republican—publicly stood united in favor of a piece of legislation.

Despite their conservative positions on economic, poverty, and foreign policy issues, donors are somewhat more liberal on social and cultural issues. Republican donors are divided on abortion, with a small plurality opposed to a ban on abortion except to save the life of the mother.[2] Large majorities of Democrats and independents oppose an abortion ban. In this sense, the donors' opinions are closer to the views of partisan voters' than to the candidates to whom the donors contribute (Jelen and Wilcox 2002).

A plurality of Republican donors would ban gays from teaching in public schools, but a large majority of Democrats and a plurality of independents favor allowing gays to teach. More than 95 percent of all Democratic donors would prefer women to have equal roles in business, industry, and government. A large majority of Republican donors support equal rights for women, but a remarkable 22 percent either oppose gender equality or are neutral.[3] Finally, a majority of Republicans think that the country has gone too far in helping minorities, but a large majority of Democrats disagree.

TABLE 3.5 THE INFLUENCE OF PARTISANSHIP ON SIGNIFICANT DONORS'
EVALUATIONS OF SELECTED GROUPS

	Democrats	Republicans	Independents
Chamber of Commerce			
Warm	10%	51%	39%
Neutral	24	22	31
Cool	66	27	31
National Rifle Association			
Warm	2%	27%	20%
Neutral	5	19	13
Cool	93	54	67
Christian Coalition			
Warm	2%	31%	17%
Neutral	3	18	14
Cool	95	51	68
Conservatives			
Warm	7%	82%	39%
Neutral	16	11	33
Cool	77	7	29
Sierra Club			
Warm	66%	11%	22%
Neutral	20	14	32
Cool	14	75	45
National Organization for Women			
Warm	52%	7%	20%
Neutral	21	12	21
Cool	27	81	59
AFL-CIO			
Warm	39%	2%	8%
Neutral	30	4	17
Cool	32	94	75
Liberals			
Warm	71%	1%	16%
Neutral	19	9	25
Cool	11	89	59
(N)	(311)	(510)	(199)

Note: Chi-square tests indicate that all differences between donors are statistically significant at p<.001. Some columns do not add up to 100 percent due to rounding.
Source: The Congressional Donors Survey.

The diversity of contributor opinions is also evident in their evaluations of different prominent social, economic, and political groups. Each party is a loose coalition of different groups that sometimes cooperate or compete with a party or with one another. Many Americans take political cues from the positions of prominent political groups. This is particularly the case for individuals who are sophisticated in their political knowledge (Sniderman, Brody, and Tetlock 1991). A group-oriented "likability heuristic" allows citizens to quickly make sense of the political world. They perceive the positions of groups they like and dislike and use this information to formulate their own positions.

We asked contributors to rate a series of political and ideological groups on feeling thermometers, ranging from zero degrees (very cold) to 100 degrees (very warm). Cool ratings are those below 40, warm are above 60, and neutral are between 40 and 60. The congressional donors' partisanship has a significant impact on their evaluations of the groups. Republican contributors are warm toward the Chamber of Commerce, representing mainstream businesses, and generally cool toward the National Rifle Association (NRA) and the Christian Coalition (see table 3.5). Democrats, however, are generally cool toward the Chamber and very negative toward the NRA and the Christian Coalition. Indeed, two-thirds of the Democratic donors rate both the NRA and the Christian Coalition at zero degrees—the coldest possible score, whereas approximately one in five Republicans also rate these conservative groups at zero.

Democratic contributors are generally warm toward the Sierra Club and slightly warm toward the National Organization for Women (NOW). They are neutral toward the AFL-CIO—an organization that has historically comprised a major part of the Democratic coalition. This reinforces the picture of Democratic congressional donors having a very different orientation toward economics than the party's core electoral supporters. Not surprisingly, Republican donors are cool toward each group. Their antipathy does not approach the Democratic feelings toward the NRA and the Christian Coalition: half or fewer Republicans rate NOW or the AFL-CIO at zero degrees, and only one-third rate the Sierra Club that coldly.

INTRAPARTY FACTIONS

Just as there are divisions within parties among voters and candidates, there are divisions within parties among contributors. We identified two distinct groups of Democratic donors, two distinct groups of Republicans, and one group of centrists based on their positions on issues and evaluations of groups.[4]

Democratic donors cluster into two groups. The first group, comprising 22 percent of all donors and more than two-thirds of the Democrats, are committed to advancing the party's traditional liberal positions. These "traditional Democrats" support an expansion of the welfare state, are opposed to tax cuts and defense spending, and hold liberal positions on cultural issues, particularly on abortion and women's equality in the workplace. They are actively involved in the Democratic Party and are most likely to be members of environmental organizations. These donors, when compared to all other donors, have the most favorable opinions of the Democratic Party, the Sierra Club, NOW, and the AFL-CIO, and they are the most opposed to the Republican Party, the Chamber of Commerce, the NRA, and the Christian Coalition.

The second group, the "new Democrats," make up 10 percent of the donor pool and slightly less than one-third of the Democrats. They are more supportive of increased defense spending than the traditional Democrats, and they are likely to include donors who belong to a business organization. Although these donors have favorable opinions of the Sierra Club and NOW, they are not as supportive of these groups as are the traditional Democrats. The new Democrats have moderately favorable opinions of conservatives, the Chamber of Commerce, and even the Republican Party.

The largest group of GOP donors is the "consistent conservative Republicans," comprising 30 percent of all donors and more than 60 percent of all Republicans. These donors favor less government intervention and regulation of the economy. They are conservative on some cultural issues such as affirmative action and homosexual rights, but they are more divided on other social issues, such as abortion and women's equality in the workplace. Conservative Republican donors are likely to be involved in a business organization and have the most favorable opinions of conservatives, the Chamber of Commerce, the NRA, and the Christian Coalition.

The "moderate Republicans," constitute about 19 percent of all donors and 40 percent of all Republican contributors. They are conservative on issues such as taxes, health care, environmental protection, and defense spending. They favor free trade but are liberal on issues such as abortion and moderate on affirmative action and gay rights. These donors generally have negative feelings toward groups that are identified with the socially conservative wing of the GOP, such as the NRA and Christian Coalition. They also have negative feelings toward most Democratic-leaning groups.

The remaining donors are "centrists." They have no partisan attachments and are ideologically moderate. The centrists comprise nearly 20 percent of all donors. They have moderate views on most economic and cultural issues. They are likely to belong to a business organization and have favorable opinions of the Chamber of Commerce, but they have a moderately favorable opinion of the Sierra Club. They have unfavorable opinions of the NRA, NOW, the AFL-CIO, and the Christian Coalition.

Summary

Congressional donors are more diverse than the popular stereotype. Although some, like Tom Smith are investors who contribute to advance their economic self-interest, others, like Harriet White, are interested in broader public goods, such as a clean environment. Still others, like Dick Jones are interested in the social side of giving—supporting a candidate who has been a long-time friend and meeting with others at a fundraising event.

Many donors possess more than one motive for contributing, and these motives vary by gender, age, religion, income, and party. Although investors have attracted the greatest attention for their pursuit of narrow economic gains, ideological donors make the most contributions. They also contribute with the greatest frequency, especially to presidential and senatorial candidates. Intimates, on the other hand, are the most likely to volunteer to work together with others on a political campaign.

The donor pool does not speak with one voice on public policy. Most Democratic donors take liberal positions on policy issues, whereas Republicans are conservative on economics but divided on social issues. Party affiliation is also a source of division among donors in their evaluations of many, but not all, political groups. Republicans are very warm toward conservatives and business associations and generally warm toward the Chamber of

Commerce, but many are cool toward the NRA and the Christian Coalition. Democrats are cool toward the Chamber and hostile to the NRA and the Christian Coalition, and they are generally warm toward the Sierra Club and the NOW.

However, even Democratic donors are not warm toward the AFL-CIO, and this points to the limitations of pluralism among contributors. Although most Democratic donors favor increased social programs and affirmative action, nearly all are affluent whites. The few union members in the donor pool are members of government workers' or teachers' unions, and they are motivated primarily by purposive and not economic motives. These findings paint a mixed picture of contributors: they are more diverse than the portrait painted in chapter 2, but there are few who have experienced the realities that confront blue-collar union workers, the poor, members of the Christian Coalition, and other groups that do not contribute to congressional candidates. In short, donors do not sing with one voice, but there are many voices missing from the choir.

chapter 4

Candidates, Donors, and Fundraising Techniques

Donors constitute one side of the fundraising equation; candidates constitute another. Successful candidates for Congress must persuade large numbers of Americans to contribute to their campaigns.[1] Many of these potential donors can imagine spending their money in more enjoyable ways, and thus the task facing candidates, and their fundraising teams, is not an easy one. Although there exists a ready pool of habitual donors, and another group that gives in some elections, these donors do not usually press themselves upon the candidate to offer contributions. As a result, candidates must wage a campaign to raise money that is just as complicated as the campaigns they wage to win votes.

The campaign for resources, like the campaign for votes, involves strategic targeting, message development, personal and impersonal communications, and mobilizing the support of diverse groups of supporters (Herrnson 2000). Fundraising consultants market themselves by claiming expertise in each of these areas and asserting their unique ability to combine the precise message and technique needed to successfully raise the most from each potential contributor. The science of fundraising involves rigorously assessing candidate and donor characteristics, and determining what the two groups have in common. The art of fundraising concerns finding an efficient way to bring the groups in contact with one another so a campaign contribution can change hands.

Most consultants begin by assessing the candidate's fundraising assets and liabilities, consider the potential donor's political activism, partisanship, motives, and financial wherewithal, and try to select the most appropriate solicitation method for achieving a positive response. Finance directors consider a number of issues when developing a fundraising strategy. A major factor is whether the candidate is an incumbent, challenger, or open-seat contestant. If the candidate is an incumbent, they consider whether he or she serves on a committee that is attractive to prospective donors, or whether he or she is a congressional party leader. They also evaluate whether the candidate is sufficiently associated with a cause to attract donors who care about such issues.

A different set of questions emerge when assessing a prospective donor: Is the donor someone who regularly gives to candidates? Is the person motivated by material, purposive, or social incentives? Does he or she work in politics or regularly contact elected officials? Is the potential donor a strong partisan or hold strong views on controversial issues, such as abortion rights? Does he or she routinely make campaign contributions or ask others to contribute to candidates, party committees, or PACs? Additional considerations involve the potential donors' education, income, age, and religion, among other things.

Finally, a good fundraiser asks: What do I need to do to get this person to contribute to my candidate? Do I need to have someone who knows the donor make the solicitation or will a stranger do? Does the solicitation have to be in person or involve a fundraising event, or is a telephone call or a direct-mail piece sufficient?

In this chapter, we provide an overview of the assets and liabilities different kinds of candidates bring to the money chase. We also describe how candidates develop and carry out their fundraising operations. Next, we analyze the fundraising process from the perspective of those who finance congressional elections, discussing the relationship between donor characteristics and the number and types of solicitations they receive. Finally, we identify which candidates solicit which donors.

INCUMBENCY ADVANTAGES

Incumbents have tremendous fundraising advantages over other candidates. They possess a stable set of financial supporters to whom they can routinely turn for large contributions. They can use their influence over the policy process to leverage contributions from individuals and organized groups whose interests are affected by government action or inaction.

Also, incumbents possess lists of financial supporters from previous races and maintain records of the solicitation techniques to which they responded. A base of loyal supporters and a list of tried-and-true fundraising appeals provide incumbents with the ability to raise seed money they can use to scare off potential primary- or general-election opponents or finance further fundraising efforts (Green and Krasno 1988; Box-Steffensmeier 1996; Herrnson 2000). Many incumbents use funds left over from the previous election to maintain a fundraising operation or skeletal campaign organization between campaigns.

Donors have significant incentives to contribute to incumbents. Given the high reelection rates enjoyed by members of Congress, access-oriented investors find it profitable to support incumbents. Most intimates are inclined to support incumbents because their fundraising events guarantee donors the opportunity to rub elbows with people in power rather than those who are involved in an uphill struggle to win it. Ideologues also have strong incentives to contribute to incumbents in danger of losing their seats. Because incumbents have voting records and a history of championing an issue, their commitments to various causes are better known than are the commitments of challengers and open-seat candidates.

Challengers find themselves on the opposite side of the coin from incumbents in the campaign for resources. The same factors that operate as assets for incumbents function as liabilities for challengers. Most challengers do not own contributor lists or develop fundraising appeals that are as well-honed as those possessed by incumbents. Challengers possess no influence over the legislative process in Congress, which discourages individuals and groups motivated by material concerns from contributing to them. Few challengers enjoy the celebrity status that motivates some of the donations given by intimates. Even those challengers who are strongly identified with "hot" issues, such as abortion rights or the environment, must compete with other candidates, including other challengers, to raise money from ideologically motivated individuals and groups. Indeed, few challengers have the visibility to raise significant sums from PACs, parties, or individuals who make large contributions. Many invest their own money to jumpstart their own campaigns and signal the seriousness of their candidacy (Biersack, Herrnson, and Wilcox 1993; Herrnson 2000; Jacobson 2001).

Moreover, most challengers do not do much to build their visibility as candidates until relatively late in the election cycle. Most do not begin to implement their campaign plans until about a year prior to the election. Although the small number of challengers who have previously held elected office can ask their past donors for contributions, few, if any, carry over surplus funds from their previous races. Their late start in fundraising means that most must struggle to raise the seed money they need to collect the resources that must be used to fuel the rest of their campaign. Challengers rarely organize fundraising operations that are anywhere nearly as professional or reliable as those assembled by their opponents (Herrnson 2000). Some are able to draw on their professional networks to help them raise funds, but challengers with political occupations provide more lucrative sets of fundraising contacts than do others.

Perhaps the biggest handicap that challengers face is potential donors' expectations that they will lose. Most individuals and groups that contribute to political campaigns are aware that well over 90 percent of all House challengers and 75 percent of all Senate challengers lose in the general election. These overwhelming odds plague challengers' fundraising efforts. In order to overcome the low expectations that handicap them at the outset of the election season, congressional challengers need to be able to point to at least one aspect of their candidacy that differentiates it from the others. Most try to make the case that their political experience or the competitiveness of their seat will result in their being one of the few candidates who will defeat an incumbent. A few challengers try to argue that their races give contributors the unique opportunity to knock off an incumbent who occupies a position of power or is an ideological extremist. Others try to use their gender, race, or ethnicity as a means for raising money from donors with whom they share one or more demographic characteristics. In a competitive race, party and interest-group leaders will also help a candidate appeal to ideologues, investors, and intimates (Herrnson 2000; Jacobson 2001).

Candidates for open seats possess some of the advantages of incumbents and some of the disadvantages of challengers. Their odds of victory are not as favorable as those enjoyed by members of the former group or as slim as those who belong to the latter. Elections for open seats attract substantial numbers of candidates who have acquired significant political experience (Canon 1990; Herrnson 2000; Maisel, Stone, and Maestas 2001). Given the astronomically high reelection rates for sitting incumbents, many qualified politicians prefer to wait until a House member runs for higher office, retires, or dies before declaring their candidacies. This option poses fewer political risks than waging an uphill battle to defeat an incumbent in a primary or general election (Kazee 1994; Maisel, Stone, and Maestas 2001). As a result, open-seat races are usually competitive enough to attract the attention of the individuals and groups who make large contributions, and most open-seat candidates are usually skilled enough to collect significant sums from them.

Although incumbency is probably the most important electoral advantage any congressional candidate can enjoy, there are additional factors that influence fundraising. Some incumbents have certain strengths that make them better fundraisers than others. Likewise, some challengers and open-seat candidates are prolific fundraisers who sometimes outdistance even the typical incumbent. The assets and liabilities that each incumbent, challenger, and open-seat candidate brings to a campaign can determine how much money it raises. Solicitations become particularly important because candidates often use them to market their strengths to prospective donors.

TARGETING SOLICITATIONS

Candidates want to raise as much money as possible, and they attempt to capitalize on their strengths by soliciting a large pool of prospective donors. Yet, asking for a contribution can have costs. Solicitations can be expensive, sometimes exceeding 12 percent of a typical House candidate's entire campaign budget (Herrnson 2000). A broadly targeted prospecting letter will lose far more money than one directed to a more carefully tailored list.

When members of a candidate's fundraising team ask business associates for contributions, they are spending personal capital. The solicitor risks embarrassment if the request for a contribution is for a candidate to whom the associate is hostile. A mistargeted contribution request can erode an individual's ability to ask an associate for a contribution in the future. For this reason, fundraisers attempt to focus their solicitations on donors who would seriously consider giving to their candidate.

Candidates who hold institutional positions, such as party leadership and committee leadership posts, including chairmanships and ranking-member positions, often solicit the executives of companies with business before their committee. Incumbents often time their fundraising events to coincide with upcoming committee deliberations or with other legislative action, and materially minded donors often feel that they have little choice but to give. Corporate PAC directors are invited to sponsor tables at fundraising events, and the implication that giving will help protect their interests is often strong. Small wonder that so many business donors state that they often give so that their business is treated fairly.

A legislator's congressional voting record can also serve as a fundraising asset. House members who are recognized for their ideological fervor can sometimes tap into networks of political activists when raising money. Given that the motives of these contributors involve electing legislators who share their views, conservative Republicans and liberal Democrats may have more success raising funds from significant donors than moderate legislators. Indeed, it is quite common for candidates with strong ideological appeals to identify those who share their views and craft special communications to capitalize on their common beliefs.

When Barbara Boxer sought reelection to the U.S. Senate, she raised large sums through the mail. Her campaign mailed to members of EMILY's List (a PAC that raises money for pro-choice Democratic women candidates), to Jewish donors, and to other cultural liberals. It would have made little sense for Boxer to mail letters to members of the National Rifle Association, because she had a strong record of support for gun control. In contrast, when Senator Jesse Helms sought reelection, his campaign would be far more likely to mail to NRA members than to members of the National Women's Political Caucus. Policy moderates, on the other hand, seldom find that moderation is an asset in raising money from purposive donors. Direct-mail letters seldom ask citizens to send money on behalf of a compromise position on abortion or gun control, because moderation does not usually go hand-in-hand with the kind of strong, purposive motivation needed to produce a contribution (Godwin 1988).

Demographic characteristics are routinely used to target solicitations. In response to the perception that women traditionally had more difficulty raising campaign funds, organizations such as EMILY's List were formed to help them target contributors. Groups such as the National Organization for Women, WISH List, and other pro-women groups, have developed programs to create networks of women contributors and stimulate their donations to female candidates for the House, Senate, and other offices (Thomas 1994, 1999; Rozell 1999; Day, Hadley, and Brown 2001; Francia 2001). Political consultants also have compiled fundraising lists based on age, ethnicity, race, and religion.

Political parties have identified a set of supporters who are especially willing to give in competitive elections (Herrnson 1988; 2000). If a challenger is competitive, the party will help them target solicitations to those most likely to respond. If a challenger receives a positive assessment from organizations that handicap congressional elections—or in publications such as the *Cook Political Report*, the *Rothenberg Political Report*, and *CQ Weekly*—they can quote these in fundraising letters or telemarketing scripts.

Campaigns, however, must carefully consider not only whom to ask and what strengths to publicize, but how to ask for money. Some donors, particularly those who give the largest sums of money, often expect a personal call from the candidate. These donors, as one professional fundraiser explained, "like to be stroked" (Bocskor 1998). Some donors want to get something for their money and are likely to respond to solicitations that involve events such as formal dinners and informal backyard barbecues (Webster et al. 2001). Other donors are responsive to appeals made through direct mail and telemarketing. How donors ask for money is thus often as important as whom they ask for money.

Raising Money with a Personal Touch

Campaign fundraising usually starts at home. In most cases, it begins with a candidate writing a check to jump-start the campaign. A personal investment, often in the form of a loan, is a sign that a nonincumbent is serious about running for office. Without it, many potential donors will not make a contribution. Next, most nonincumbents turn to family, friends, and professional associates for the seed money that is needed to get the campaign off the ground. Incumbents rarely have to reach in their own pockets or those of close friends and family members for their early funds because they often have money left over from their previous campaigns or can call on the support of previous donors when they start filling their campaign chests. Seed money is important in that early contributions are often plowed back into fundraising efforts that stimulate additional contributions (Biersack, et al. 1993; Krasno, Green, and Cowden 1994). Candidates may also turn to family, friends, and associates to help them form finance committees, which are a virtual necessity for any campaign that is serious about raising money.

Finance Committees

Most finance committees have broad-based memberships that enable them to tap into a wide spectrum of donors. Ideally, the finance chair is a well-connected individual who will devote many hours to raising money. Many Republican House candidates choose a local business leader for their finance chairs; many Democrats select a local union leader or civic activist. Candidates from both parties often select prominent attorneys for their finance chairs. The remaining committee members are chosen because of their ability to tap into different economic, social, religious, racial, or geographic communities for financial support. Democratic and Republican candidates in the New York City area often recruit Wall Street financiers, doctors, lawyers, and individuals involved in the city's arts community. Prominent Italians, Jews, Catholics, Hispanics, and Asian-Americans are also recruited. Many Democratic candidates, and some liberal Republicans, recruit members of the gay and lesbian communities to serve on their committees. Candidates from rural areas often recruit farmers, NRA members, and church leaders to help them raise money.

The growth of the national economy of campaign finance has encouraged some candidates, primarily incumbents, to appoint nationally recognized contributors to their finance committees. These individuals are often Washington, D.C., lobbyists, Hollywood celebrities, and prominent individuals who reside in New York City, Hollywood, Austin, or the nation's other major centers of wealth. They solicit large contributions from local residents as well as friends and associates located across the country. Most politicians and fundraisers are shrewd enough to go where the money is when trying to fill a campaign chest (Sorauf 1992).

Finance committee members are recruited for reasons besides their stature in the communities they represent. Good finance committee members are organized, able to motivate others, and not easily discouraged by rejection. Nancy Bocskor, a prominent fundraiser for congressional Republicans, maintains that insurance agents, car dealers, and others in the sales professions make ideal finance-committee members because they have aggressive, assertive, "bounce-back" personalities and are used to making dozens of sales pitches before accomplishing their goals (Bocskor 1998). They also have extensive Rolodexes and personal organizers, and they recognize that their client list is a source of potential contributors and their contributor list provides them with a source of future clients. Although most of these individuals are capable of writing very large checks, their ability to raise money is more important than their ability to contribute it.

Candidates who anticipate having to wage very expensive campaigns, such as those located in districts with high-priced media markets, form a pyramidlike structure composed of many levels of fundraising committees. Members of the candidate's main finance committee form separate finance committees, which they chair. Each member of the team is asked to raise a certain sum and to solicit associates and friends. It is common practice to solicit those with ties to your business (Brown et al. 1995). As one fundraiser explained, "You start with the people who can't say no to you." In some cases, members of these committees form an additional layer of finance committees below them.

Personal Solicitations

Once a finance committee is organized, it begins to pursue its mission: to raise a large amount of money in a finite period. Campaign fundraisers are often very successful at mobilizing donors through solicitations. Solicitations give the potential donor a stake in the race, providing information about the candidate, some endorsements from prominent politicians or local celebrities, negative information about the opponent, and an indication of how the donor's money will be spent.

Most fundraising consultants believe that negative fundraising appeals are more successful than positive ones so they write scripts that inform potential donors of what they would lose if the opponent won (Godwin 1988). They also believe it is important to convey evidence indicating that the race will be competitive and the contribution well spent. Veteran Democratic fundraiser Kimberly Scott, President of Conklin Scott, a Washington consulting firm, explains that her scripts for House candidates in close races will typically state that the Democratic Congressional Campaign Committee has made the race one of its most targeted campaigns and has established a fundraising goal that must be met by next week in order for the campaign to receive the maximum level of support from the party, and that the campaign needs to raise a certain amount (for example, $35,000) by this Friday in order to make a media buy (of, say, $70,000) to air its latest TV advertisement (Scott 1999).

Other donors are involved in "personal-acquaintance" networks (Brown et al. 1995). These networks are often based on professional contacts and involve lobbyists. For the largest contributors, campaigns make appeals through face-to-face requests. In-person solicitations allow donors an opportunity to discuss their concerns with the campaign. In addition, they are often a useful first step for establishing personal contact with a candidate or with a high-ranking campaign aide or legislative staff member who is responsible for the donor's issues.

Talking to Strangers

Solicitations that are not between personal acquaintances often take the form of ads in newspapers or magazines. Some are printed alongside news articles or commentaries; others appear in the section of the periodical that lists announcements of upcoming events. Senate challenger Charles Schumer has advertised some of his fundraising events in the *Village Voice*, a free newspaper that is widely read by residents of New York City. A small number of candidates have experimented with making fundraising appeals during radio and television appearances and in their electronic mass media advertisements. The best-known of these was former Democratic Governor Edmund "Jerry" Brown's frequent announcements of the toll-free telephone number for his 1992 presidential nomination campaign. During the 1998 elections, more than 70 percent of all House and Senate candidates experimented with collecting campaign funds in cyberspace by including fundraising appeals and instructions for contributors on their Internet web pages (Dulio, Goff, and Thurber 1999). Because they are untargeted, it is impossible to learn how many individuals actually receive impersonal solicitations or calculate their success rates.

Campaign professionals also are successful at mobilizing donors using direct-mail and telephone solicitations. The keys to success in direct-mail fundraising and telemarketing are a good donor list and a compelling sales pitch on script. The list should be composed of individuals who are sympathetic to the candidate, agree with his or her issue positions, and have a history of contributing to campaigns or other political, social, or economic causes. Most incumbents and experienced nonincumbents possess a reliable "house list" from their previous campaigns. This is one of their most valuable assets because past donors have a high probability of supporting the candidate again. According to one estimate, house lists have an average success rate of 10 percent, but they have been known to break the 20-percent mark, ensuring the campaign considerable profit (Godwin 1988).

The typical House incumbent has a house list of between 20,000 and 30,000 donors, which is periodically updated by the campaign staff (Sabato 1989). Senate incumbents' house lists are usually much larger. Party leaders in both chambers possess house lists with contributors that number in the hundreds of thousands. Candidates can also purchase, rent, or occasionally obtain for free, lists from other politicians, interest groups, organizations, magazine publishers, or professional list brokers. Some party committees and interest groups lend their lists to candidates with the proviso that the candidates turn over their donor lists to the organization after the election (Herrnson 2000).

Prospecting for donors from some other organization's list is not very economical. Letters usually cost between $3.00 and $4.00, and response rates for prospecting are usually low. The fact that a candidate shares a group's position does not ensure a good return rate. Environmentalists may be happy to join the Sierra Club or subscribe to *National Geographic*, and many gun owners are pleased to pay dues to the NRA or buy a subscription to *Guns and Ammo*, but most of these same individuals are unwilling to contribute to an unfamiliar candidate who claims to champion environmentalist or anti-gun-control positions. Similarly, relatively few readers of the *New Republic* or the *Weekly Standard* are likely to contribute to candidates who espouse the ideologies expressed in those periodicals. Candidates who prospect from lists furnished by other organizations usually enjoy a success rate of only 1 or 2 percent, which is significantly lower than is achieved with a house list (Godwin 1988). However, once someone has given, they are added to the candidate's house list and therefore go on to give more regularly (Bocskor 1998).

The best direct mail uses highly charged rhetoric to play on the recipient's emotions, gives the recipient an idea of how his or her contribution will be used, stresses the need for the recipient to respond immediately, and provides that individual with the materials needed to take action (for an example, see figure 4.1). Direct mail that forcefully advocates cherished values, and characterizes the candidate as locked in a fierce battle to

SENATOR X

Dear Fellow Citizen,

I'm hoping you will indulge me for a few moments while I tell you a story.

I believe you'll find that my story will say a lot about the dangerous state of American democracy today and about what all of us who share progressive values must do to restore the health and vibrancy of our political system.

With **the Right wing now effectively dominant throughout** the Federal government—the Presidency, the Congress, and the Supreme Court—the challenge to the humane values we share is more formidable than ever.

If you're feeling anything like me, it must be difficult for you to control the anger and frustration you feel. Even worse, some of the people I've talked to in the past few months are losing hope of a better life for our children.

We must not let that happen. Those of us who support the interests of working families simply cannot yield to hopelessness. **We must transform our anger into a renewed struggle to advance the agenda of working families.**

With just a few swing states going our way, **the next election can enable Democrats to continue to** set the agenda and to refocus on the issues at the center of most Americans' lives.

I ask you to join me again in pursuing this vision.

Please respond as quickly and as generously as you are able. Your gift will help give me the chance to provide leadership on Capitol Hill on some of the most contentious and critical issues of our day.

Here is my promise to you: I will do everything in my power to remain worthy of your support.

Sincerely,

[candidate's first name signed]

[candidate's full name]
United States Senator

FIGURE 4.1

protect them, is the most likely to succeed. This mail exaggerates opponents'positions and often attacks their characters. For example, pro-life candidates often portray themselves as fighting a war against godless baby killers in their direct-mail solicitations. Pro-choice candidates, by contrast, argue that they are not only battling to protect a woman's right to protect herself from a dangerous or unwanted pregnancy, but they are fighting to prevent the extremist forces of the radical right from turning back the clock and relegating women to second-class citizenship. Inflammatory rhetoric and fear are potent tools for raising contributions from ideologically motivated donors (Sabato 1989; Godwin 1988).

Direct mail is a print medium, and if it is not properly packaged and embellished, prospective donors are unlikely to open the envelope or read beyond the first line of text. For this reason, professional fundraisers use a variety of gimmicks to engage and motivate potential donors. The best direct-mail pieces look like telegrams, use brightly colored decorative stamps, or have some other distinctive packaging. They are printed on high quality personal or business letterhead and feature realistic signatures and handwritten postscripts. They are personally addressed and repeat the recipients'name throughout the body of the text. Press clips, questionnaires, or other enclosures are included to draw the recipients'attention. The contribution card lists a variety of donation amounts and often confers titles, such as patron, supporter, or friend, to persons who contribute at different levels. Some cards invite donors to volunteer in the campaign or participate in some other way. These efforts are intended to make prospective donors feel like they are part of an important cause, which is useful in convincing them to make a contribution.

E-mail solicitations promise to be an important fundraising tool in the future. Few Internet-access companies sell their subscribers' e-mail addresses to organizations that intend to use them for solicitations, but this is not true of all private organizations. E-mail lists of individuals who share a candidate's issue concerns are a potential source of monetary and volunteer support, especially among today's computer-literate youth. Perhaps the greatest appeal of e-mail is that the actual delivery of the solicitation is free. Of course, the tradeoff is that e-mails from unknown senders are rarely appreciated. Mass e-mails, often referred to as "spam," result in the functional equivalent of tossing an unopened piece of direct mail in the trash or hanging up on a telemarketer as soon as one recognizes the nature of the call.

E-mail solicitations are not yet widely used, but this technology can deliver a message that is virtually identical to that included in direct mail. Press clips and pictures can be placed in electronic files that are attached to the main body of the message. Individuals can respond to questionnaires using the reply command on their e-mail system and can even make their donations by typing in their credit card number. The main differences between "snail-mail" and e-mail solicitations are that the former comes on printed paper and includes a reply envelope, and the latter can be responded to, deleted, or forwarded with minimal physical effort. In addition to e-mail, some candidates have begun to raise money directly from their Web sites. The advantage of this approach is that donors go to the site and contribute on their own volition. In addition, people who contribute over the Internet do not fit the typical donor profile—they are younger, less partisan, and concerned with different issues. This method of solicitation has the potential to expand the donor pool to those who are otherwise unlikely to give (Powell et al. 2001). The disadvantage is that few individuals donate online to congressional candidates, even though this approach has been successful for insurgent candidates for the presidency, such as John McCain in 2000.

Telephone solicitations differ from those delivered electronically or by mail in that there is live interaction between the persons who make and receive the solicitations. Telemarketing requires a much shorter, livelier message, and its success depends heavily on the abilities of the person actually making the telephone call. Lacking signatures, press clips, and other gimmicks, telemarketing depends almost exclusively on the quality of the message and the caller's voice, and the accuracy of the targeting list.

Telemarketing solicitations are more expensive and typically have lower response rates than direct mail. Professional telemarketers usually charge several dollars per call. People do not like being asked for money at home, and few congressional candidates have enough name recognition to inspire an individual to listen to a telemarketer's fundraising pitch. Moreover, most telephone solicitations require a mail followup because donors often do not like to give their credit-card numbers over the telephone. Nevertheless, telemarketing offers some advantages. It puts the caller in immediate contact with the prospective donor, whereas most direct mail is immediately thrown into the trash. Telemarketing solicitors can negotiate with prospective donors about the amount of their contributions. Telemarketers can gain instant feedback about the potency of their message or rapidly change it in response to changing circumstances, whereas the substance of a direct-mail appeal is fixed once it is in print. Finally, campaigns use volunteers to make most of their telephone calls.

FUNDRAISING EVENTS

Fundraising events typically involve combinations of personal and impersonal solicitations both to individuals who know the prospective donors and to complete strangers. Finance committee members who help plan events invite their friends and acquaintances to come to the event and invite others to do likewise. In addition to using these personal invitations extended to friends and strangers, fundraising consultants use lists of previous donors to the candidate and lists of previous donors obtained from other candidate sources to invite strangers. Strangers who have previously given large contributions to congressional candidates, parties, or PACs usually receive a personal invitation. Others generally receive an invitation in the mail.

Events have the benefit of attracting volunteers, generating press coverage, energizing the candidate and campaign staff, and, if held early enough in the election season, discouraging opposition. Events also make it possible for members of the host committee, which organizes them, to ask prospective donors to bring friends to the event, thereby increasing the candidates' donor base. For an event to be successful, it must be both economical and fun. Theme parties are very popular. Republican House member Sherwood Boehlert capitalizes on the fact that his upstate New York congressional district includes Cooperstown, home of the Baseball Hall of Fame, by hosting an annual baseball-theme fundraising event. Boehlert invites baseball players and celebrities, such as former New York Yankees' champion shortstop Phil Rizzutto and Baltimore Orioles' star pitcher Jim Palmer, to the events. The players become a major drawing card for the event, and many contributors come to meet them, have their pictures taken, and get their baseballs autographed. Because the theme of the event is baseball, the campaign serves hot dogs and other ball park food, which enables it to limit its catering costs to roughly $7.00 per person (Bocskor 1998).

Likewise, Congressman Jack Quinn of Buffalo hosts a "Buffalo Bills Night" in which donors typically give $50 for an inexpensive meal of

Buffalo wings and "Genny" (Genesee) Cream Ale. These low-cost events collect smaller donations but usually raise substantial funds and media attention for candidates (Bocskor 1998). Former Congresswoman Susan Molinari of Staten Island used the birth of her daughter Susan Ruby as an occasion to solicit funds. Other congressional candidates hold house parties (see figure 4.2), Italian nights (featuring pizza), and farm breakfasts (where they serve ham and eggs). Birthday celebrations are very popular. Events that feature movie stars and political leaders are also very successful.

Some fundraising events are actually two events in one. The first event is a dinner or some other small gathering that allows large contributors to meet with the candidate or special celebrities in a fairly intimate setting. The second, and much larger, event can have dozens or even hundreds of small and medium donors milling about in a large hall, listening to the candidate make a formal address, or being entertained by music. Both kinds of fundraising events typically satisfy the motives of two types of donors. Investors view these events, especially the smaller ones, as an opportunity to increase their visibility with the candidate; some raise the possibility of later meeting with the candidate to discuss

---

You are cordially invited to join
the Host Committee for

Candidate "X"
Democrat for Congress

Countdown to Victory Party!

Wednesday, September 4th
6:30 – 8:30 pm

At the home of
[host "xx"]
[address]

Patron	*$1,000*
Benefactor	*$500*
Sponsor	*$250*
Friend	*$125*

Please RSVP by enclosed envelope or call [phone number]

FIGURE 4.2

a policy concern. Intimates enjoy the social aspects of the events, including having the opportunity to see and be seen with the candidate and other important people. Fundraising events usually have less appeal to ideologues, who view campaign contributions as a way to elect more people who share their views to Congress, and who are rarely concerned with having proximity to people in power or trying to influence the legislative process.

If at First You Don't Receive, Ask, Ask Again

To make effective use of their time, fundraisers look for potential donors from the lists of those who have given before. Past donors have weighed the opportunity costs of a contribution against the benefits that the contribution might entail, and they have elected to contribute. They are more likely to give than are citizens who have never contributed to a campaign. As a consequence, most members of the donor pool are asked to give by more than one candidate.

Not surprisingly, those who contribute the most in any single election cycle are likely to be solicited by many candidates in the next election. Fewer than one in five occasional donors were asked by more than six candidates, as opposed to the more than 40 percent of habitual donors (see figure 4.3). One politically involved donor explained his frustration with the deluge of solicitations he receives. "Because I am so active and give a lot of money to many candidates, I am constantly solicited. It really has gotten out of hand. These days politicians are scared and they think they need more money to hedge against risk. They are wrong, of course."

This experience was also similar for major donors, more than 80 percent of whom were asked to give by more than six candidates. When asked to list the candidates who solicited them, several donors wrote back that there were simply too many to remember. Many respondents indicated that the same candidate had contacted them several times, using different modes of contact.

Yet not all donors receive many solicitations. Nearly one in ten significant donors were asked to give by a single candidate in 1996. A plurality were asked by no more than five candidates.

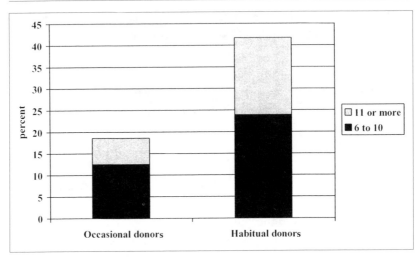

FIGURE 4.3 DONORS WHO WERE SOLICITED BY SIX OR MORE CANDIDATES
Source: The Congressional Donors Survey.

While the number of solicitations that a donor receives is partly a function of the frequency of their past giving, other factors also are likely to be important. Donors who are deeply integrated in politics or are involved in political groups should be more likely to be solicited by multiple candidates.[2] Further, those who ask others to give should be asked to give to more candidates, because of the norm of reciprocal solicitations that exists in fundraising (Brown et al. 1995). Those who hold political jobs—lobbyists, politicians, PAC directors, etc.—are more likely to be solicited than others. Those who contact Congress frequently also should be asked to give more often, primarily because they are likely to have business before Congress that makes them easy targets for fundraisers. In each case, these types of donors are likely to show up on the Rolodex and Palm Pilot contact lists of fundraisers.

It is likely that demographic variables matter as well. The wealthiest donors are likely to be asked to give more often. Wealthy citizens often give to the opera or to a local charity, and they come to the attention of fundraisers. Higher levels of education are often associated with higher rates of solicitation, even controlling for income. Those with the most education are typically professionals—lawyers, doctors, and dentists, for example—and there are professional solicitation networks already in place in these communities (Brown et al. 1995). Older donors also appear on more lists and therefore might be solicited more often.

Those who are involved in various political networks may be more likely to receive solicitations. Although the vast majority of donors are men, many of the women in our survey indicated that they gave in coordination with EMILY's List, a group that bundles contributions for female, pro-choice, Democratic candidates. It is therefore possible that women are more likely to be solicited by many candidates. Religion also may be an important factor in assessing rates of solicitations. Jewish donors may receive more solicitations than others; past research has shown strong networks of soliciting and giving in that community (Levick-Segnatelli 1994). It is also possible that evangelical Protestants receive more solicitations, because lists of evangelical donors are readily available.

In addition, individuals with certain political beliefs appear on more donor lists and therefore are probably asked to give more often. This group includes strong partisans. Party fundraisers are likely to know the strongest partisans and help candidates connect to those donors (Herrnson 2000). Finally, donors with strong convictions on hot-button issues, such as abortion, may receive more solicitations (Godwin 1988).

Results generated from an ordered probit analysis suggest that political integration is associated with the number of solicitations an individual receives (see table 4.1).[3] Those who are better educated and wealthier are asked to contribute by more candidates than are others.[4] Individuals who work in politics, frequently contact members of Congress, or regularly make political donations also are solicited with greater frequency. The same is true of those who belong to politically active networks, such as strong partisans, women, and Jews, and individuals who belong to a diversity of organizations. Motives also are significant, as donors who are motivated by purposive incentives are among the most frequent targets of contribution requests.

Political integration has a tremendous effect on the number of solicitations an individual receives. A strong partisan who routinely contributes to congressional candidates, is a member of eight or more groups, works in politics, and contacts between six or more members of Congress in a typical year is 67 percent more likely to be asked to make a contribution by six or more candidates than is an independent who does not work in politics, only occasionally makes a campaign donation, belongs to one or no groups, and never contacts a federal lawmaker.[5] Moreover, ideologues are 7 percent more likely to be solicited than those who are unconcerned with highly charged issues or broad-based concerns.[6] Political activists and

TABLE 4.1. THE INFLUENCE OF POLITICAL AND SOCIOECONOMIC FACTORS ON THE NUMBER OF SOLICITATIONS RECEIVED BY SIGNIFICANT DONORS

	Coefficient	SE
Material motives	.064	.043
Purposive motives	.075*	.041
Solidary motives	-.013	.040
Habitual donor	.372***	.088
Membership in number of types of groups	.030*	.018
Asked others to give	.096	.087
Political job	.324***	.096
Number of members contacted	.170***	.021
Woman	.219*	.100
Evangelical	-.011	.133
Catholic	.032	.105
Jewish	.433***	.137
Strong partisan	.166*	.096
Democratic partisanship	.033	.022
Education	.078**	.033
Income	.166***	.042
Refused income	.398*	.210
Age	.004	.003
Cut 1	.504	
Cut 2	1.259	
Cut 3	3.385	
Cut 4	4.225	
Log likelihood	-854.075***	
(N)	(846)	

Note: Estimates are based on ordered probit analysis. Material, purposive, and solidary motives are based on factor scores generated from survey questions that asked donors to identify the reasons they made a contribution to a congressional candidate (see table 3.2 for factor loadings). "Habitual donors" is a dummy measure and refers to those who contribute to House or Senate candidates in most elections. "Membership in number of types of groups" is the sum of the different types of organizations (out of a possible 18 choices) of which donors report they are members. "Asked others to give" refers to donors who answered that they have asked other people to make a contribution to a congressional candidate. "Political job" is a dummy measure that refers to donors who report that their job involves politics or government. "Number of members contacted" is the total number congressmen and senators that donors have contacted in the past two years. "Woman" is a dummy measure that refers to the gender of the donor. "Evangelical," "Catholic," and "Jewish" are each dummy measures that represent the religious affiliation of the donor. "Strong partisan" is a dummy measure that refers to donors who identify themselves as either a strong Republican or a strong Democrat. Democratic partisanship is a seven-point measure that reflects the donor's party identification in which 1 = strong Republican, 4 = Independent, and 7 = strong Democrat. "Education" is a five-point measure that represents the donor's level of educational attainment (1 = high school or less; 2 = some college; 3 = college graduate; 4 = some graduate; 5 = graduate degree). "Income" is a five-point measure that represents the donor's family income (1 = less than \$50,000; 2 = \$50,000–\$99,999; 3 = \$100,000–\$249,999; 4 = \$250,000–\$500,000; 5 = Above \$500,000). "Refused income" is a dummy measure that refers to donors who did not report their family income. "Age" is the donor's age.
***p<.001, **p<.01, *p<.05.
Source: The Congressional Donors Survey.

ideologues, like women and Jews, are among the most likely to be asked to make a campaign contribution because of their integration into various political communities and because their names generally appear on numerous subscription and membership lists. Campaigns often purchase these lists and make tailored appeals to attract donations from these individuals (Godwin 1988).

The donor pool thus contains a small elite group of individuals who are regularly solicited by many candidates. These donors are distinctive in their level of political integration, wealth, and other demographic characteristics. They are the first to be asked by many candidates. However, candidates generally reach well beyond this activist core when they seek to fill their campaign chests.

Who Solicits Whom?

It is clear that most solicitations are made by someone the donor knows. That someone is not just anyone. Fundraisers must know not only how to approach prospective donors, but who they should get to make the actual solicitation. This is why they go to such great efforts to organize finance committees.

When asked to tell us how likely they would be to give when asked by various types of personal acquaintances, 69 percent of all donors said they often or occasionally respond to solicitations by personal friends or relatives. This confirms the importance of the personal touch. Similarly, all groups of donors are likely to respond to solicitations from candidates but much less likely to respond to solicitations by campaign aides. Often a phone call from a candidate can "close the deal" in a way that no other solicitor can manage.

In general, intimates are more likely to indicate that they would respond positively to all types of solicitors, with the sole exception of requests made by fellow business associates. Investors are distinctive in their responses to coworkers and business associates. Among investors, there was a strong correlation between saying that they would give when asked by a business associate, and saying that they would give when asked by someone to whom they felt they could not say no. This is consistent with our earlier discussion of solicitation networks built around business obligations.

Donors in the survey listed up to three candidates who successfully solicited a contribution and up to three candidates who unsuccessfully asked for money. Some respondents did not fill in candidate names, and others only reported those to whom they had given but not those that they refused. Donors appear to remember the solicitations they responded to more than those they refused, and thus a large majority of reported solicitations were successful.

Investors are more likely to be solicited by incumbents than are ideologues or intimates (see table 4.2). For example, 72 percent of the solicitations investors report receiving from House candidates are from incumbents, as opposed to 62 percent for ideologues, 68 percent for intimates, and 59 percent for incidental donors. Only incumbents can provide material benefits, and they are also more likely than challengers and open-seat candidates to host lavish fundraising events. In contrast, nonincumbents who embrace ideological causes often use their issue positions to appeal for money from their ideological soul mates. Indeed, nonincumbents may be uniquely able to attract donors with strong purposive motives because they have not yet had their pure ideology sullied with the realities of political compromise.

Investors are more likely to be solicited by members of relevant committees in the House, but there is no difference in the Senate. This may reflect the fact that committees are more important in passing legislation in the House than in the Senate (see, e.g., Davidson and Oleszek 2002). Senators serve on multiple committees, which helps to explain the higher rate of committee solicitations in that chamber.

Ideologues receive more out-of-district solicitations from candidates for the House and out-of-state solicitations from aspirants for the Senate. Nearly all significant donors are solicited by local candidates—more than 80 percent received a solicitation from a House or Senate candidate in their district or state.

Investors are the most likely to receive solicitations from candidates of the other party. Ideologues are more likely than investors to get in-party solicitations, but intimates are the most likely to be solicited in-party. Donors appear to enjoy socializing more within their party than within the other party. Finally, the average ideological distance between donors and the candidates who solicited them is smaller for ideologues than for investors and intimates.

We examined the patterns of solicitation for the major donors as well, but the number of cases was often too small for us to make definitive conclusions. There were a couple of major differences, however, worth not-

TABLE 4.2. THE CANDIDATES WHO TARGET SOLICITATIONS TO IDEOLOGUES, INVESTORS, INTIMATES, AND INCIDENTALS

	Investors	Ideologues	Intimates	Incidentals
Percentage of solicitations from:				
House incumbents	72%	62%	68%	59%
Other House candidates	28	38	32	41
Senate incumbents	59%	52%	62%	52%
Other Senate candidates	41	48	38	48
On relevant House committee	12%	4%	5%	4%
Other House candidates	88	96	95	96
On relevant Senate committee	7%	7%	6%	5%
Other Senate candidates	93	93	94	95
House party leader	14%	9%	10%	13%
Other House candidates	86	91	90	87
Senate party leader	17%	17%	20%	12%
Other Senate candidates	83	83	80	88
Within House constituency	32%	26%	31%	36%
Other House candidates	68	74	69	64
Within Senate constituency	58%	49%	54%	53%
Other Senate candidates	42	51	46	47
House, same party	55%	70%	78%	55%
Other House candidates	45	30	22	45
Senate, same party	59%	70%	72%	63%
Other Senate candidates	41	30	28	37
Average ideological distance				
House	1.31	1.14	1.27	1.08
Senate	1.30	1.11	1.25	1.14
Number of solicitations	(772)	(1,412)	(715)	(272)

Source: The Congressional Donors Survey.

ing. First, the major donors were likely to report more solicitations from incumbents. In addition, major donors were more likely to report solicitations from outside their state and across party lines.

Taken together, these findings suggest that candidates target their solicitations to donors who would at least consider making a contribution. The characteristics we measure do not capture all the subtleties of the targeting decision. For example, it may be quite rational for a Republican committee chair in the House to target a Democratic donor who is interested in the policy agenda of his committee. The data understate the degree of targeting by sophisticated campaign professionals. An important idiosyncratic factor is whether the fundraiser personally knows the donor.

IT'S ALL IN HOW YOU ASK

We asked each respondent to report which candidates had solicited him or her in the preceding election cycle. For each candidate, the respondent reported whether or not he or she was solicited by someone they knew, and whether they were invited to an event. We also asked whether they were solicited in person, over the phone, or by mail. Some donors reported receiving a number of different types of solicitations, of which some were associated with the same event. Campaigns make initial contact by mailing someone an invitation to an event, then a campaign aide or fundraising consultant often follows up with a telephone call. Indeed, nearly one in five candidates who the donors report having solicited them had asked them to an event and solicited them in person, over the phone, and by mail. Clearly solicitors have learned the virtues of persistence.

Most of the solicitations reported by the donors came from an acquaintance, but intimates were far more likely to have been solicited by someone they knew than were ideologues (see table 4.3). Seventy-four percent of the intimates report they were asked to make a contribution by someone they knew, as opposed to 60 percent of the ideologues. The overall recall rate of solicitations from acquaintances is doubtlessly much higher than the recall rate of solicitations from strangers, making it impressive that four out of ten solicitations that ideologues remembered were made by someone they did not know.

How donors are asked to contribute is also important. Ideologues and incidental donors were the least likely to report being asked in person and the most likely to report being solicited through the mail. The figures for mail probably underestimate the number of solicitations received because direct-mail solicitations are not very memorable and many are tossed in the trash unopened. Intimates and investors are more likely to be asked in person. Investors are more likely to be asked to give over the phone than ideologues or intimates. Intimates are the most and ideologues are the

TABLE 4.3. THE MODES OF SOLICITATION THAT CAMPAIGNS USE TO RAISE
MONEY FROM IDEOLOGUES, INVESTORS, INTIMATES, AND INCIDENTAL DONORS

	Investors	*Ideologues*	*Intimates*	*Incidentals*
Asked by someone you know	69%	60%	74%	66%
Asked in person	54	38	43	37
Asked by mail	65	71	67	72
Asked by phone	37	30	34	43
Invitation to event	65	55	67	60
Personal solicitation				
By someone known	48%	35%	37%	36%
By someone not known	6	4	7	1
Impersonal solicitation				
By someone known	22%	25%	38%	30%
By someone not known	25	37	19	32
Number of solicitations	(772)	(1,412)	(715)	(272)

Note: Columns do not add up to 100 percent because some donors received multiple types of solicitations.
Source: The Congressional Donors Survey.

least likely to be invited to an event. The impersonal solicitations that ideologues receive are especially likely to be from outside their constituency or state, and this makes an invitation to an event unlikely. Moreover, fundraisers have learned that ideologues will frequently give even without an event, thus increasing the net proceeds from the contribution.

We combined some of these items to form four categories: solicited in person by someone the donor knew, solicited in person by a stranger, solicited impersonally (by phone or mail) by someone the donor knew, and solicited impersonally by a stranger. We separately identified those solicitations that were invitations to an event. To understand who is solicited how, we estimated a series of logistic regressions to predict each mode of solicitation. The results provide a nuanced picture of the fundraising process.[7]

Candidates and fundraisers begin their campaign for resources by personally contacting donors they know. As indicated earlier, first they pick the low-lying fruit. Donors who they are fairly certain will make a contribution—such as strong previous supporters, habitual donors, individuals who themselves belong to the networks of donors who solicit others, and wealthy donors—are contacted in person (see table 4.4, column 1). Next, they proceed to call on interest groups or political leaders to connect them with the leaders' supporters. Some congressional leaders escort challengers, open-seat candidates, and junior legislators to meetings with potential donors (Herrnson 1988, 2000). This makes politically active donors, who frequently contact members of Congress and belong to many advocacy groups, targets for personal solicitations. The driving force behind these contacts is personal relationships. In these situations personal relationships override all donor motives.

TABLE 4.4. THE INFLUENCE OF POLITICAL AND DEMOGRAPHIC FACTORS ON THE METHOD OF SOLICITATION

	Personal Donor Knows	*Personal Stranger*	*Impersonal Donor Knows*	*Impersonal Stranger*	*Events*
Material motives	-.016	.049	-.049	.089	-.009
Purposive motives	.017	-.054	-.077*	.163**	-.098*
Solidary motives	-.010	.194**	.161***	-.317***	.200***
Habitual donor	.401***	.443*	.204*	-.854***	.165*
Membership in number of types of groups	.072***	-.048	-.012	-.064**	.085***
Asked others to give	1.069***	.411*	-.320**	-.871***	.417***
Political job	.069	-.686**	.319***	-.397***	-.072
Number of members contacted	.068***	-.063	-.012	-.079***	.076***
Woman	-.434***	-1.508***	.117	.666***	.320**
Evangelical	.149	1.512***	-.331*	-.587***	-.113
Catholic	-.031	.578**	-.201*	.166	-.024
Jewish	.119	—	.097	-.196	-.732***
Strong partisan	.088	-.013	-.334***	.185	.126
Democratic partisanship	.021	-.068	-.080***	.077**	-.034
Education	.088*	-.349***	-.035	.080*	.005
Income	.168***	-.139	.059	-.199***	.093*
Refused income	1.421***	-.179	-.376	-1.062***	.879***
Age	-.040***	-.022**	-.009**	.063***	-.011***
Constant	-1.031	.265	.117	-3.041	-.066
(N)	(2,967)	(2,967)	(2,967)	(2,967)	(2,967)

Note: Estimates are based on logistic regression analysis. See table 4.1 for variable definitions. Jewish donors had to be dropped from the personal-stranger analysis because they provide perfect predictions.
***p<.001, **p<.01, *p<.05.
Source: The Congressional Donors Survey.

Second, candidates and their finance directors try to tap into members of the donor pool who they do not know personally. Often referred to as "dialing for dollars," challengers, open-seat candidates, and even junior members of the House telephone individuals who have a history of supporting like-minded candidates or causes. Habitual donors and individuals who routinely ask others for contributions are also targeted for these types of solicitations (see table 4.4, column 2). Hiring a finance committee director is often critical to making these contacts.

Third, campaigns often send fundraising letters to a broader set of individuals who know the candidate or someone who is helping the candidate raise money. These contacts frequently take place when congressional or interest-group leaders write to potential donors on behalf of the candidates. Officeholders are almost always on these lists. Each of these types of solicitation relies on some personal element that leads campaigns to target intimates (see table 4.4, column 3). These solicitations are primarily targeted at ideologues and are done through direct-mail funding. This allows campaigns to identify potential donors who shape the policy view of the candidate.

Fourth, campaigns contact individuals they have never met. Ideologues are prime targets for direct-mail solicitations from candidates they do not know personally. Direct-mail fundraising is the major reason for this. Most direct-mail fundraisers specialize by party and some specialize by cause. Most will only work for candidates of one party and some will only work for candidates who belong to one or another wing of their party because their lists are tailored to ideologically motivated donors. Candidates and partisan fundraisers often rent contributor lists from candidates and interest groups, who share their political philosophy. This explains the deluge of impersonal requests that arrive in their mailboxes. Democrats and women, many of whom embrace liberal causes, are particularly vulnerable to being buried in piles of fundraising mail from congressional campaigns (see table 4.4, column 4). Senior citizens also are often targeted because they are very responsive to fundraising letters, as they are to many other kinds of solicitations. Indeed, senior citizens are among the only donors who will read a six-page fundraising letter. Some donors even enjoy reading fundraising letters. As one ideologue admitted, "I like to read junk mail. It really pumps you up. It's like, our side is on the march and the other side is scum. I know this is silly, but it makes me want to contribute to the cause."

As noted earlier, fundraising events involve combinations of personal and impersonal solicitations. These events strongly appeal to intimates, who are routinely invited to them (see table 4.4, column 5). One donor explained, "Almost all of my donations occur at events. I don't have to know the candidate personally, but I like hearing them talk, answer questions, and present themselves." Donors who engage in political activity that frequently occurs in a social context—namely, those who belong to many groups, solicit contributions from others, and frequently contact their representatives—are more likely to be invited to events than others. Wealthy donors and those who frequently contribute also receive many invitations to political events.

How do these patterns and relationships translate into the types and numbers of different kinds of solicitations that donors receive? The exam-

TABLE 4.5. THE INFLUENCE OF SIGNIFICANT DONORS' MOTIVES ON THE PROBABILITY OF RECEIVING SOLICITATIONS

	Strong Material Motives	Strong Purposive Motives	Strong Solidary Motives
Personal solicitation from someone the donor knows	47%	49%	48%
Personal solicitation from a stranger	5	4	6
Impersonal solicitation from someone the donor knows	32	30	44
Impersonal solicitation from a stranger	12	14	5
Solicitation for an event	70	66	79
(N)	(2,967)	(2,967)	(2,967)

Note: Probability estimates are based on the likelihood of a solicitation occurring for a typical donor. The probability estimates are based on a multivariate logit model that controls for habitual donors, the number of groups the donor belongs to, whether the donor asked others to contribute, whether the donor holds a job in politics, has contacted a member lof Congress, and other socioeconomic factors such as education, income, age, gender, religion, and partisanship. Donors with "strong" material motives are in the 90th percentile for material motives but fall in the bottom 10 percent for purposive and social motives. Donors with "strong" purposive motives are in the 90th percentile for purposive motives but fall in the bottom 10 percent for material and solidary motives. Donors with "strong" solidary motives are in the 90th percentile for social motives but fall in the bottom 10 percent for purposive and material motives.
Source: The Congressional Donors Survey.

ple of a typical hypothetical donor sheds further light on these results.[8] Individuals who are highly motivated to contribute—whether investors, ideologues, or intimate—are solicited personally by someone they know. Those who are in the ninetieth percentile on each of these motives are almost 50 percent more likely to receive this type of solicitation than those in the bottom 10 percent (see table 4.5). Motives have little impact on the likelihood of being personally solicited by a stranger; the difference in likelihood between the most highly motivated and least highly motivated donors is approximately 5 percent. Those who are the most strongly motivated by social considerations are especially likely to receive an impersonal solicitation from someone they know, such as a letter from a friend inviting them to a fundraising event. Ideologues and investors are more likely than intimates to receive impersonal solicitations from strangers, primarily direct-mail and telemarketing calls.

Summary

Campaign fundraising requires more planning than simply asking individuals for contributions. One size does not fit all when it comes to raising money. Fundraising requires candidates to carefully consider the strengths and weaknesses of their campaigns, the kinds of individuals who are likely to support them, and the solicitation methods that will lead a prospective donor to part with some money. Incumbents are better positioned than other candidates to raise money because they possess lists of financial supporters from previous races and have influence over the policy process. Also, candidates who stake out strong stances on ideologically charged issues usually raise significant sums when they target like-minded donors.

Some fundraising techniques work more effectively for some kinds of candidates and donors than for others. Some contributors expect personal requests from a top aide in the campaign or from the candidate. Other donors are less interested in a personal request but expect something for their money, such as an invitation to a formal dinner, informal backyard barbecue, or some other fundraising event. Campaigns must be persistent and continuously ask for money by crafting solicitations that highlight the candidate's strengths and appeal to the interests of the donor. The most successful fundraisers are those who are discriminating in the solicitation methods they use to appeal to donors who possess different motives.

Indeed, not all donors are the same, nor are all candidates the same. These unique differences influence how campaigns must tailor their solicitations, and often determine which fundraising approaches are most effective. As we will demonstrate in the next chapter, variations in the characteristics of candidates and the characteristics of donors affect not only solicitations, but also who contributes to whom and how much money candidates ultimately collect for their campaigns.

chapter 5

The Contribution

When donors receive solicitations from candidates, they must decide whether or not to contribute. This decision may be made slowly. For example, a donor might discuss an invitation to an event with a spouse or friend. The decision also might be made quickly, using a standing rule, as when a potential donor drops a solicitation letter in the trash unopened. Sometimes a quick initial decision to contribute requires later consideration, such as when a friend asks a donor face-to-face to give to a candidate and the donor needs to consult with a spouse about how much to contribute.

Even when the decision to contribute is made quickly, it often reflects more carefully considered decision rules that can be rapidly applied to a particular solicitation. This is especially true for habitual donors. Donors may consider how difficult it is to say no to a specific solicitor, or the implications of their decision for their personal relationship to the candidate. They might consider whether the candidate could help or hurt their business, or whether the candidate represents their views on abortion or taxes. Donors may consider whether the candidate is from their party or in a close election.

We examine several questions concerning the decision to contribute to congressional candidates. First, what criteria do significant donors use in making their contribution decisions? When deciding whether to respond to a solicitation, do donors focus more on the characteristics of candidates such as ideology, incumbency, and institutional power, on characteristics of the contest such as whether it islikely to be close, and whether it is local, or on the identity of the solicitor? Second, do different types of donors consider different factors in deciding whether to give? Do investors focus more

on committee assignments, ideologues more on policy positions, and intimates on the nature of the solicitation, or are the patterns more complex?
Third, what factors influence to which candidates donors contribute?
Fourth, what factors are most important in determining which candidates
will raise the money from individuals? Incumbents obviously raise more
money than challengers, but what factors help determine which incumbents raise more, and which challengers do better than others?

CRITERIA FOR CONTRIBUTING

Although there have been many studies of voting decisions and how political parties and PACs choose to distribute their funds (see, e.g., Eismeier and
Pollock 1988; Baker 1989; Clawson, Neustadtl, and Scott 1992; Herrnson
1988, 2000), little is known about how individual donors choose among
congressional candidates. Presidential donors have a variety of motives that
influence their contribution decisions (Brown et al. 1995). We similarly expect that donor motives will influence congressional contributions.

In the last chapter, we demonstrated that different types of donors are
asked to give by different types of candidates and in different ways. Donors
also differ somewhat in the types of solicitors to whom they were most
likely to say yes. We anticipate donors will vary in their contribution decisions as well, based on their motives for political involvement. In some
ways, we expect the decision rules adopted by investors and ideologues to
resemble those of business and ideological PACs. For example, we expect
investors to contribute to members of congressional committees that over-
see policies that affect their business.

Investors also may care about the policy positions and party of the candidate, but these should be secondary to the ability of the candidate to provide particularized benefits to their business. Investors seek access to policymakers who can help their business. A liberal Democratic House
member may not be a business donor's first choice, but if that Democrat
sits on a key committee and has in the past supported amendments or
changes in mark-up sessions that help the company, the incumbent may receive a contribution. In general, such donors should be more likely to give
to incumbents and to single out those who serve on committees of special
relevance to their business. Investors care about candidates' stances on particular issues, but these issues are more likely to be narrowly economic—

special tax matters, specific regulations, or government contracts. Investors also may contribute because of their business ties to the solicitor, and in those cases, the characteristics of the candidate may well be irrelevant.

Ideologues care about the policy positions of candidates, but this may manifest itself in different ways—they should be more likely to contribute to candidates who are close to their ideological views or who belong to their party. Some ideologues also care about the political views of the opponent. Many interest groups target incumbents for defeat who have the worst records on their issues, and urge their members to support the challenger even if the challenger's positions are not ideal. The League of Conservation Voters, for example, has for years identified the "Dirty Dozen" members of Congress who have the worst environmental records (Mundo 1999). Because public policy frequently depends on the ideological composition of Congress, ideologues should be more willing than some other donors to give to nonincumbents and target their money to candidates in close races.

Intimates may give because of their personal ties with a candidate or solicitor, or because of the nature of the event to which they are invited. They should be more likely to give to candidates of their party, because those events will be more socially satisfying. They also may be more likely to give to incumbents or to candidates for the Senate, who can provide more extravagant events. Intimates may be especially likely to give to local candidates because of their stronger ties to community leaders.

Sources of Information

Before donors can apply their criteria for contributing, they must acquire information about individual candidates and their elections. A number of sources are available to prospective donors, including political newsletters and newspapers, as well as information provided by political campaigns and organizations, such as political parties, labor unions, business associations, religious groups, and other ideological groups (Biersack et al. 1994; Herrnson 1988, 2000). Which of these sources is most important in helping donors decide to which House or Senate candidate to contribute?

Significant donors are most likely to maintain that newspapers are helpful in their contribution decision, with almost 69 percent reporting it is an important source (see table 5.1). Campaigns are the next most common source at 66 percent, followed by business groups, ideological or issue groups, political newsletters, party organizations, religious groups, and labor unions. Donors with different motives make varying use of these sources. Information from business groups, for example, is particularly important to investors. Investors are often motivated by business concerns, so it is not surprising that they turn to business groups for information in helping them to decide which candidates to support. Ideologues are more likely than are other donors to name ideological groups as an important source of information. One women noted, "I read NARAL and NOW newsletters; Emily's List, Wish List, and so forth. Virtually 95 percent of my donations are a result of them." Another ideologue added, "I pay a lot of attention to groups like EMILY's List, the AFL-CIO, and the [state] Democratic party. They can tell me which races are hot and which ones are not."

Finally, incidentals are the least likely to regard candidates and campaigns as an important source of information, whereas ideologues and intimates are the most likely to report party organizations as an important source of information. These patterns suggest that while most donors turn to some common sources of information, such as newspapers, to help them with their contribution decision, donor motives influence their reliance on other information sources.

TABLE 5.1. INFORMATION SOURCES SIGNIFICANT DONORS USE
WHEN MAKING CONTRIBUTION DECISIONS

	All	*Investors*	*Ideologues*	*Intimates*	*Incidentals*
Political newsletters	31%	30%	34%	34%	23%
Labor unions	7	7	7	8	4
Candidates/campaigns	66	64	69	70	57
Religious groups	13	10	15	15	6
Newspapers	69	66	69	69	72
Business/industry / trade groups	45	65	31	50	34
Party organizations	28	23	30	33	23
Issue/ideological groups	43	35	58	41	22
(N)	(983)	(248)	(357)	(236)	(142)

Note: Chi-square tests indicate that differences between donors are statistically significant at p<.001 for business/industry/trade groups, and for issue/ideological groups—and at p<.05 for candidates, campaigns, religious groups, and party organizations. Columns do not add up to 100 percent because donors could receive information from multiple sources.
Source: The Congressional Donors Survey.

Reasons to Contribute

Individuals' reasons for making a political donation have a major impact on the candidates to whom they choose to contribute. What factors do donors consider when selecting which House or Senate candidates to support? When this question is put to significant donors, investors emerge as the most likely to indicate that business concerns, such as ensuring that

TABLE 5.2. Ideologues', Investors', Intimates', and Incidentals' Reasons for Making a Contribution to a Congressional Candidate

	Investors	Ideologues	Intimates	Incidentals
Candidate's position on specific issue	39%	39%	35%	21%
Candidate's liberalism-conservatism	62	88	60	55
Candidate's party	22	37	35	22
A group I respect supports the candidate	12	15	14	4
Candidate's opponent is unacceptable	58	51	50	33
Candidate is likely to win the election	9	5	9	1
Candidate is in a close race	20	36	20	13
So my business will be treated fairly	58	10	20	1
Candidate is friendly to my industry or work	63	10	21	4
People in my line of work are giving	10	—	6	—
Candidate's seniority, committee leadership position	10	4	11	8
Asked by someone I don't want to say no to	12	5	16	7
Candidate is from my district or state	71	62	69	70
I know the candidate personally	49	42	56	47
Asked by someone I know personally	28	21	35	10
Involves an event that I want to attend	2	2	12	—
(N)	(248)	(357)	(236)	(142)

Note: The designation ``—`` indicates less than 0.5 percent. Chi-square tests indicate that all differences between donors are statistically significant at p<.01. Figures represent the percentages of donors who report that each reason is always important. Columns do not add up to 100 percent because donors often cited more than one reason for making a contribution.

Source: The Congressional Donors Survey.

their business is treated fairly or that the candidate is friendly to their industry, motivate their giving (see table 5.2).[1] Indeed, sizable majorities of investors maintain that business matters are always important to their contribution decisions. Investors are less likely than ideologues and intimates to say that they care about the party of the candidate, whether the candidate is in a close race, or that their contributions are motivated by group endorsements.

Investors are much less likely than ideologues to state that ideology always matters, but they mention candidates' stances on specific issues about as often as do ideologues. In this case, the specific issue is likely to be something important to their material well-being, such as taxes, subsidies, regulations, or trade issues that affect their businesses. On other items, investors' decision-making criteria fall between those of ideologues and intimates. Investors are more likely than ideologues to report that it is always important whether they are asked to give by someone whom they know or don't want to refuse, but these considerations are even more important to intimates. Of course, the nature of the pressure is different. Investors fear that refusing to give might endanger future business considerations, whereas intimates fear damaging a social relationship. Among investors, the person they least want to refuse is a business associate. As for intimates, they least want to turn down solicitors they know personally. They are especially likely to give when asked by a friend.

Ideologues are likely to say they always care about a candidate's stance on a specific issue, the candidate's general ideology, and their party. These donors are slightly more likely than others to indicate that they rely on group endorsements and much more likely to say that they care whether the candidate is in a close race. They also are the least likely to care about business matters, or about who solicits them.

Intimates are especially likely to indicate they always consider whether the invitation is an event, but only 12 percent of intimates state that this is always important. Fully 50 percent of intimates state that an invitation to an event is sometimes important compared to just 15 percent of all other donors. More than three-fifths of intimates respond that events at least sometimes matter, compared with only 19 percent of ideologues, 16 percent of investors, and 10 percent of incidentals. Clearly, events do motivate intimates to give. Intimates also are the most likely to consider whether they know the candidate personally and whether they are asked by someone whose request they do not want to say no to or reject.

Incidentals, who do not express any clear motives for contributing, are not distinctively more likely to indicate that any factor influences their decisions. However, they are significantly less likely to mention several potential sources of influence, such as group endorsements, an unacceptable candidate, or the treatment their business gets in the legislative process. Incidentals are the least likely to mention any factors except whether the candidate is from their district or they know the candidate. This suggests that incidentals are enticed into making a contribution by the specific qualities of the individual candidates.

WHO GIVES TO WHOM?

A donor could theoretically give to any congressional candidate. Some donors only give to one. The most active donor in our study contributed to about forty candidates—just over 5 percent of all candidates.[2] The decision to contribute to any particular candidate is an extremely unlikely event.[3] To explore the decision to contribute we created a separate record for every possible pairing of contributors and candidates. For each donor the odds of giving to any particular candidate were quite small. Of the 505,155 pairings of donors and candidates, only 1,260 resulted in contributions—just 0.2 percent.[4] The odds of any single donor giving to any particular candidate are therefore infinitesimal, and we are seeking factors that might increase these odds to the merely minuscule. We use rare-events logit to predict whether a donor gave to a particular candidate (see, e.g., King and Zeng 1999).[5]

As expected, donors are more likely to give to candidates with whom they share a party affiliation (see table 5.3, column 1). The likelihood of a contribution increases 6.7 times when the donor and the candidate belong to the same party, controlling for various political and socioeconomic factors. Indeed, fully 75 percent of all contributions are made from a donor to a candidate of the same party. Furthermore, donors are more likely to give to candidates who share similar ideological views. Donors are more likely to contribute to candidates in close races and to incumbents.

Geography is the most important factor influencing contribution decisions. Donors are much more likely to give to candidates in their state or district. The likelihood of a contribution to a House candidate increases by roughly 33 times when the candidate runs for office in the congres-

TABLE 5.3. THE EFFECTS OF PARTISANSHIP, POLITICAL CONDITIONS, AND
SOCIOECONOMIC FACTORS ON INDIVIDUAL CONTRIBUTIONS TO HOUSE AND
SENATE CANDIDATES

	All Candidates		House Candidates		Senate Candidates	
	Coefficient	SE	Coefficient	SE	Coefficient	SE
Party agreement	1.93***	.17	1.90***	.22	1.97***	.28
Political independent	1.45***	.17	1.38***	.22	1.57***	.28
Ideological similarity	.34***	.05	.31***	.06	.40***	.08
Competitive race	.43***	.04	.44***	.05	.38***	.10
Incumbent	1.00***	.12	1.07***	.15	.70**	.25
Open seat	.35*	.17	.51*	.23	.03	.27
House candidate in same constituency	3.50***	.13	3.49***	.13	NA	—
House candidate in same state	4.07***	.14	4.08***	.14	NA	—
Senate candidate in same state	5.26***	.14	NA	—	5.27***	.14
Senate candidate	2.12***	.16	NA	—	NA	—
Senate candidate not up for reelection	-1.14***	.17	NA	—	-1.19***	.24
Donor follows congressional committee	.15	.12	.28*	.15	-.16	.22
Candidate is member of committee that donor follows	.82***	.21	1.14***	.25	.41	.32
Habitual donor	.43***	.09	.37***	.11	.51***	.15
Income	.20***	.04	.14**	.06	.30***	.07
Refused income	.47*	.22	.39	.29	.63	.25
Constant	-13.99		-13.66		-12.13	
(N)	(505,155)		(431,970)		(73,185)	

Note: Estimates are based on rare-events logit analysis. "NA" refers to coefficients
that were not included in the model because they are not applicable. "Party agreement"
is a dummy variable that represents when the donor and candidate had the same party identification. "Political Independent" is a dummy measure that refers to donors who report their
party identification as purely Independent. "Ideological similarity" designates the proximity
on a 7-point scale between the ideological views of the donor and those of the candidate in
which a high score of 7 indicates identical views for the donors and candidate. "Competitiveness" is a 4-point variable in which the high score indicates a very competitive race and the
low score indicates an uncompetitive race. The measure is based on forecasts from *CQ Weekly*
(October 19, 1996, pp. 2964–2969). "Incumbent" is a dummy variable that reflects whether
the candidate ran for office as an incumbent. "Open-seat" is a dummy variable that reflects
whether the candidate ran as an open-seat candidate in the general election. "House candidate in same constituency" is a dummy measure that designates when the individual donor
resides in the same congressional district as the House candidate running for office. "House
candidate in same state" is a dummy measure that designates when the individual donor
resides in the same state as the House candidate running for office.

(continued on next page)

(continued from previous page)
"Senate candidate in same state" is a dummy measure that designates when the individual donor resides in the same state as the Senate candidate running for office. "Donor follows Congressional committee" is a dummy measure that designates whether the donor closely follows the activities of any particular House or Senate congressional committee.
"Candidate is member of comittee that donor follows" is a dummy measure that reflects a match between an individual donor who identified closely following a particular committee and a member of Congress who served on this mentioned committee. See table 4.1 for definitions of "habitual donor," "income," and "refused income."
*p<.05, **p<.01, ***p<.001.*
Source: The Congressional Donors Survey and the Federal Election Commission.

sional district in which the donor resides. For Senate candidates, the likelihood of a contribution increases by roughly the same amount when the candidate runs for office in the donor's home state.

Moreover, about three-fourths of all contributions are made to a candidate within the state, and one-fourth is made to a House candidate in the donor's district. Among all contributions to House candidates, fully 70 percent are either to a candidate in the donor's local district or in a neighboring district. More than half of all donors gave to at least one candidate in their House district, nearly half gave to at least one Senate candidate from their state, and more than one-third gave to at least one House candidate in their state but not from their district—most of whom were candidates in neighboring districts.

Donors also are more likely to contribute to candidates who serve on committees that the donor follows closely. Donors were particularly likely to monitor the House Ways and Means Committee and the Senate Finance Committee and to contribute to their members. These committees' tax-writing authority gives particularistic benefits that are of special interest to investors. Donors are also more likely to give to Senate candidates than to House candidates but are less likely to give to senators who are not up for reelection in that year.

Donors consider different factors for House and Senate candidates (see table 5.3, columns 2 and 3). Incumbency matters more in House elections, probably because many Senate challengers already hold office and are formidable fundraisers, whereas most House challengers lack commensurate experience and skills. Donors weigh committee assignments more heavily when making contributions in House contests than in Senate contests. The threat of extended debate and the lack of a germaneness requirement for amendments to bills allow Senators who do not serve on the committee to have a bigger say on the content of legislation. Negotiations outside of the committee structure are also more common in the Senate (Sinclair 2000). However, party and ideological similarities between donors and candidates are more important in contribution decisions involving Senate candidates because those elections more frequently center on broader ideological issues.

Do donors who possess different motives contribute to different types of House candidates? Investors are most likely to support House incumbents (see table 5.4). Investors also give more often to candidates in close races than to other candidates because they almost never contribute to sure losers. Investors made just 2 percent of their contributions to losing candidates in races that were deemed uncompetitive compared to 9 percent of all ideologues and intimates and 13 percent for

TABLE 5.4. THE EFFECTS OF PARTISANSHIP, POLITICAL CONDITIONS, AND SOCIOECONOMIC FACTORS ON INDIVIDUAL CONTRIBUTIONS TO HOUSE CANDIDATES

	Investors		*Ideologues*		*Intimates*	
	Coefficient	SE	Coefficient	SE	Coefficient	SE
Party agreement	1.36***	.35	2.33***	.46	2.31***	.52
Political independent	1.11***	.33	1.78***	.47	1.68***	.55
Ideological similarity	.16*	.10	.35***	.09	.50***	.14
Competitive race	.26**	.10	.60***	.08	.22*	.12
Incumbent	1.37***	.31	.94***	.22	1.22***	.37
Open seat	.69	.50	.48	.30	.72	.61
Same constituency	3.50***	.26	3.40***	.23	3.53***	.29
Same state	4.02***	.24	3.85***	.22	4.66***	.33
Donor follows congressional committee	.28	.25	.45**	.23	.19	.39
Candidate is member of committee that donor follows	1.34***	.35	.16	.51	1.14*	.56
Habitual donor	.18	.21	.40**	.18	.57**	.25
Income	.08	.09	.21**	.09	.22	.13
Refused income	-.02	.58	.61	.46	.75	.70
Constant	-11.82		-14.54		-15.55	
(N)	(106,722)		(168,432)		(85,668)	

Note: Estimates are based on rare-events logit analysis. See table 5.3 for variable definitions.
*p<.05, **p<.01, ***p<.001.
Source: The Congressional Donors Survey and the Federal Election Commission.

incidental donors. It is also striking that investors are the only set of donors to give more often to candidates who serve on the committees that they follow closely. The likelihood of contribution from an investor increases almost four times when the candidate is on a committee that the donor cares about. Finally, ideology is not a significant factor in explaining investors' contributions to House candidates. These results strongly demonstrate that investors' motives lead them to make contributions to candidates—mainly powerful incumbents—who are in a position to influence legislation.

Ideologues care about party agreement and ideological similarity, and they are much more likely than other donors to contribute to candidates in close races. The likelihood of an ideologue making a contribution, for example, is more than six times greater when a candidate is in a very competitive race as opposed to lopsided one. By contrast, the investors and intimates are only twice as likely to contribute in close elections than in uncompetitive ones. Ideologues are also the least likely to give to incumbents and to local candidates. As noted in chapter 3, ideologues care deeply about causes and view elections as their primary means for influencing the governmental process. Electing members who share their views is the most effective way to advance issues—such as abortion rights or gun owners' rights–that these donors care about. Gaining access to unsympathetic members of Congress is of little use because these legislators are unlikely to change their minds.

Finally, intimates are more likely to give to candidates who share their party and ideology. Like most individuals, intimates appear to prefer socializing with likeminded people. Intimates also are more likely to give to House candidates from their state or congressional district because these are the candidates they typically know best. Nevertheless, local giving is not exclusive to intimates. Regardless of motives, donors are roughly thirty times more likely to contribute to a candidate from their home district or state. Contributing to local candidates clearly provides all types of donors with the benefits they seek, but for intimates contributing is mostly about mixing socially with people from their local area with whom they share common values.

The factors that influence contributors to candidates for the upper chamber are similar to those for the House, but because the results are based on a small number of very different races the results of our analysis are merely suggestive. Investors are the only group of donors who are not more likely to contribute to Senate candidates who have similar ideological views. Ideologues are more likely to give to Senate candidates who share their ideology, who are in close races, and who are up for reelection in a given election cycle. Ideologues are especially likely to care about candidates who are both ideologically similar and who are in close races. Intimates are surprisingly the most likely to consider party agreement, and they are as likely as ideologues to worry about general ideological agreement. Intimates also are more likely to give to candidates who are not in competitive elections, probably because their contributions are motivated by friendship, loyalty, and other social concerns rather than ideology or influence.

Spreading the Wealth

Most significant donors contribute to only a few candidates; however, some give to many. More than 90 percent of the congressional donors gave to three or fewer candidates, but, as noted earlier, one donor gave to forty candidates in 1996. More than half of the donors gave $500 or less, but two gave more than $30,000 apiece over a two-year period. One donor contributed nearly the legal maximum of $50,000 to congressional candidates over the course of the 1996 election cycle.

Donors who contribute to six or more candidates constitute a tiny portion of the donor pool, but they do account for a greater share of the actual money given. About 8 percent of the significant donors give to six or more candidates, but they account for 34 percent of the money these individuals contribute. If donors vary so much in their levels of giving, what factors lead some donors to give so much more money, and to so many more candidates? One would anticipate that wealthier donors would contribute to more candidates and that they would give more money. Donors who contribute large sums would be expected to be deeply enmeshed in the nation's political networks.

Which donors contribute to the most candidates? We use ordered probit analysis to estimate the political and social sources of contributing (see, e.g., Long and Freese 2001).[6] Contacting many members of Congress is associated with giving to more candidates (see table 5.5). Contacting is associated with contributing and contributing is associated with contacting, making causal inferences difficult. As expected, habitual donors, those who ask others to give, and wealthier donors (and those

TABLE 5.5. THE EFFECTS OF DONOR MOTIVES, POLITICAL CONDITIONS, AND SOCIOECONOMIC FACTORS ON THE NUMBER OF CANDIDATES RECEIVING CONTRIBUTIONS FROM SIGNIFICANT DONORS

	Coefficient	*Standard Error*
Material motives	-.078[*]	.045
Purposive motives	.087[*]	.047
Solidary motives	.003	.044
Habitual donor	.599[***]	.108
Membership in number of types of groups	.039[*]	.020
Asked others to give	.175[*]	.102
Political job	.094	.106
Number of members contacted	.042[*]	.011
Woman	.168	.113
Evangelical	.192	.149
Catholic	-.063	.124
Jewish	.294[*]	.141
Strong partisan	.051	.107
Democratic partisanship	.032	.024
Education	.018	.036
Income	.218[***]	.050
Refused income	.861[***]	.244
Age	.006	.004
Cut 1	.348	
Cut 2	2.049	
Cut 3	4.049	
Cut 4	4.463	
Log likelihood	-853.483[***]	
(N)	(889)	

Note: Estimates are based on ordered probit analysis. See table 4.1 for variable definitions.
[*]p<.05, [**]p<.01, [***]p<.001.
Source: The Congressional Donors Survey

who refused to answer the income question, presumably the very rich) contribute to more candidates. Jews also give to more candidates, perhaps reflecting their high levels of political mobilization. Similarly, ideologues contribute to more candidates, but those with strong solidary or material motives do not.

What types of donors contribute the most money to congressional candidates? We estimated these using ordinary least squares regression.[7] Donors who contact members of Congress contribute more to congres-

TABLE 5.6. THE EFFECTS OF DONOR MOTIVES, POLITICAL CONDITIONS, AND SOCIOECONOMIC FACTORS ON THE AMOUNT OF MONEY CONTRIBUTED BY SIGNIFICANT DONORS

	Coefficient	*Standard error*
Material motives	4.22	72.75
Purposive motives	44.69	71.34
Solidary motives	-181.93**	69.96
Habitual donor	388.32**	150.44
Membership in number of types of groups	6.21	30.62
Asked others to give	371.63**	147.63
Political job	258.93	163.42
Number of members contacted	198.52***	34.59
Woman	297.62*	34.59
Evangelical	383.83	234.47
Catholic	82.95	182.14
Jewish	797.71	229.81
Strong partisan	255.60	161.68
Democratic partisanship	55.78	38.62
Church attendance	-26.76	56.78
Education	25.77	56.50
Income	651.07***	72.45
Refused income	2,015.27***	360.60
Age	3.25	5.97
Constant	-3,041.24	579.58
Adj. R-square	.20	
(N)	(817)	

Note: Estimates are based on OLS regression analysis. Church attendance is a five-point measure that reflects the frequency with which the donor attends religious services. See table 4.1 for a definition of the remaining variables.
*$p<.05$, **$p<.01$, ***$p<.001$.
Source: The Congressional Donors Survey.

sional candidates than those who contact no candidates (see table 5.6). Clearly, political contacts, whether they are initiated by campaigns that are raising money or donors wishing to touch base with legislators, go a long way in explaining the amounts individuals contribute to congressional candidates. Individuals who ask others to make contributions give about $370 more than those who never try to raise money for a candidate. Not surprisingly, habitual donors and wealthy donors contribute substantially more than others. Jews also donate more money to congressional candidates.

Candidate Attributes and Fundraising Success

Candidates care more about how much money they raise than who contributes to whom, why they give, and how much money different types of donors contribute. From the candidate's point of view, a contribution is the culmination of a courtship with an individual donor. Thousands, and in some cases hundreds of thousands, of such courtships must be consummated for the typical House or Senate candidate to amass the resources needed to mount a competitive election campaign. In this section, we aggregate the campaign finance data in order to examine the effect of different candidate attributes on the amounts they raise from individuals who contribute $200 or more.

We have argued that the amounts candidates raise depend on the different assets and liabilities they bring to political fundraising. Incumbency, which brings with it policy influence and a high likelihood of reelection, is widely considered the most important factor in determining how much money candidates raise (e.g., Jacobson 1980). Party affiliation, the competitiveness of the race, seniority, and congressional leadership posts are all assets in the money chase (e.g., Herrnson 2000; Adler 2002). Challenger and open-seat candidates' fundraising prospects are influenced primarily by the likelihood of winning the seat, which in turn is thought to depend on district partisanship, the candidates' degrees of political experience, the quality of their campaign organizations, and the opponent's strengths and weaknesses (Herrnson 1992, 2000).

Fundraising by House Incumbents

Leadership posts are among the most important factors for attracting money from individual significant donors. Party leaders raise about $383,000 dollars more than do other House members (see table 5.7). The leading House Republican fundraiser in 1996 was Speaker Newt Gingrich of Georgia, who raised almost $1.9 million in large individual contributions. Minority leader Richard Gephardt of Missouri raised a healthy $872,000 in individual contributions of $200 or more. Party leaders did similarly well in the elections that followed, including in 2002. Congressional party leaders spend some of these funds on their own campaigns, but they contribute a significant portion of them to other House candidates, particularly those in close races (Herrnson 2000). Party leaders play

TABLE 5.7. THE EFFECTS OF INSTITUTIONAL RESOURCES, PARTISAN
INFLUENCES, COMPETITION-RELATED FACTORS, AND DEMOGRAPHIC FACTORS
ON LARGE INDIVIDUAL CONTRIBUTIONS TO HOUSE INCUMBENTS

	Coefficient	Standard error
Institutional Resources:		
Party leader	382.74***	78.07
Committee/subcommittee chair		
or ranking member	28.99	26.11
Power committee	15.95	23.90
Partisan Influences:		
Democrat	-111.56*	71.61
Ideological extremism	-18.11	18.70
Democrat X ideological extremism	35.77*	27.00
Competition-Related Factors:		
Opponent is an elected official	16.34	33.30
Opponent is an unelected politician	-26.95	29.82
Expected competitiveness	-2.52	19.41
First-term incumbent	109.47***	34.98
Opponent's receipts	.20***	.05
Did not face a major-party opponent	-13.82	54.36
Demographic Factors:		
Female	-8.44	37.35
Minority	-65.15**	39.00
Constant	230.40	
Adj. R-square	.23	
(N)	(381)	

Note: Estimates are based on OLS regression analysis. Figures consist of individual
contributions of $200 or more in the 1996 elections (expressed in $1,000s). Party leaders
are the Speaker, Majority and Minority Leaders, Majority and Minority Whips, and the
Conference and Caucus Chairs. The Appropriations, Budget, Commerce, Rules, and Ways
and Means committees are coded as power committees. Ideological extremism is a four-
point variable in which a high score indicates a very conservative or liberal candidate and a
low score indicates a politically moderate candidate. Elected officials have previously held
elected office; unelected officials include party officials, political aides, political appointees,
and individuals who previously ran for Congress or have some other significant political
experience. See table 5.3 for information on competitiveness.
*p<.10, **p<.05, ***p<.01.
Source: The Federal Election Commission.

a major role in the redistribution of campaign resources because the influence and visibility they derive from their institutional positions enables them to raise a great deal of money, which they can use to help their party maximize the number of congressional seats under its control. One donor acknowledged the importance of party leaders, stating: "In my experience, candidates and party leaders are the best fundraisers. I respond to them more than other people, even close friends."

House members who possess committee leadership posts or serve on the House's five most influential committees—appropriations, budget, commerce, rules, and ways and means—have a greater impact on the substance and flow of important legislation than do other members (Deering and Smith 1997). One would think that this would make them prime targets for access-oriented major contributors. Yet, these members do not collect significantly more contributions from significant donors than do others.

Legislators' ideologies and party affiliations have a significant and synergistic impact on their abilities to raise large individual contributions. Republican incumbents raise significantly more than do Democratic incumbents, a likely result of their majority party status. Liberal House Democrats also raise more money than moderate Democrats and Republicans. Democratic candidates who most distanced themselves from Republican Speaker Newt Gingrich and the Republican Congress appear to have mobilized Democratic donors in 1996. While the incumbent's ideology is important, there is no evidence that the ideology of the incumbent's opponent has a significant impact on the incumbent's ability to raise large individual contributions. Most challengers are typically unknown to most voters and potential contributors. Challengers' issue positions are even less familiar, making their views less salient on the money chase.

Some of the factors that have a direct bearing on House members' reelection prospects have a major impact on their fundraising prospects and practices. First-term incumbents, who are among the most vulnerable of all House members, typically raise $109,000 more than more senior legislators. Incumbents, who typically collect almost three times more in total contributions than do challengers, are highly responsive to challenger fundraising. For every dollar that the typical 1996 challenger raised, the typical incumbent amassed an additional 20 cents in large individual contributions.

Members of racial and ethnic minorities raise less money than whites. This could have tremendous implications for their reelection campaigns, except that most of them hold safe seats. Female House members raise amounts of money similar to those of their male colleagues, reflecting the fact that women's campaigns have reached parity with men's in terms of their professionalism and organizational capacities (Burrell 1994; Dabelko and Herrnson 1997). Nevertheless, gender can serve as a resource in the money chase. Female House members, who comprised 11 percent of all incumbents running for reelection in 1996, collected almost 13 percent of the large individual contributions made by female donors. This amounted to 39 percent of all of their individual contributions of $200 or more. Their fundraising success, in part, reflects the efforts of EMILY's List and other women's groups in developing donor pools for female candidates (Biersack et al. 1999). Should the stimulative effects of these groups result in the number of women who make large contributions coming close to reaching parity with men, female candidates will reap huge benefits.

Incumbents who belong to other traditionally underrepresented populations, such as African Americans, Asians, Hispanics, and other racial and ethnic minorities, did not raise much money from people who shared their identity in 1996 because relatively few members of these minority groups made large individual contributions. They instead relied largely on white donors.

Former Congressman Vic Fazio, who successfully won a tenth term in 1996, exemplifies the qualities and characteristics that attract individual donations of $200 or more. Fazio served as the Democratic Caucus Chairman, the ranking member on the House Oversight Committee, and as a member of the Appropriations Committee. Fazio also faced a well-financed opponent in Republican Tim LeFever, who raised a total of almost $650,000—far above the average for a challenger. The race was further forecast as competitive, with the election leaning only slightly in Fazio's favor. These conditions and Fazio's institutional power helped him raise more than $825,000 in large individual donations (close to the $725,000 predicted by the model) and more than $2.4 million total. Fazio ultimately defeated LeFever 54 to 41 percent in the 1996 election—a result that was certainly assisted by Fazio's ability to raise substantial sums of money from individual donors.

Fundraising by House Nonincumbents

The fundraising efforts of challengers who make it into the general election are influenced by several factors, including "candidate quality" (see

TABLE 5.8. THE EFFECTS OF INSTITUTIONAL RESOURCES, PARTISAN INFLUENCES, COMPETITION-RELATED FACTORS, OCCUPATION, AND DEMOGRAPHIC FACTORS ON LARGE INDIVIDUAL CONTRIBUTIONS TO HOUSE GENERAL ELECTION CHALLENGERS

	Coefficient	Standard error
Institutional Resources:		
Opponent is party leader	70.69***	31.80
Opponent is committee/subcommittee chair or ranking member	−12.90	10.91
Competition-Related Factors:		
Elected official	63.59***	16.87
Unelected politician	27.28**	12.69
Expected competitiveness	90.01***	6.11
Partisan Influences:		
Democrat	−6.03	10.36
Opponent's ideological extremism	−12.41**	5.43
Opponent is first-term incumbent	−8.74	14.22
Occupation:		
Business	29.07**	16.57
Lawyer	29.21**	16.45
Other white-collar professional	15.22	14.17
Demographic Factors:		
Female	.93	12.96
Minority	−1.05	20.26
Constant	−52.13	
Adj. R-square	.51	
(N)	(380)	

Note: Estimates are based on OLS regression analysis. Figures consist of individual contributions of $200 or more in the 1996 general elections (expressed in $1,000s). See table 5.7 for variable definitions.
*p<.10, **p<.05, ***p<.01.
Source: The Federal Election Commission.

table 5.8). Challengers who previously held elected office or are unelected politicians—which refers to candidates who ran for office previously, served as a party official, held an appointed government position, or worked on the staff of an elected official prior to their bid for a House seat—raised significantly more individual contributions than did political amateurs (Herrnson 2000). Lawyers and business executives raise more money in large contributions than do members of other professions, such as other white-collar jobs, agricultural jobs, or blue-collar occupations.

Challengers involved in competitive races raise substantially more than do others. Challengers whose races were considered toss-ups by *CQ Weekly* (1996) raised approximately $90,000 more in large individual contributions than did those whose races were characterized as leaning toward the incumbent, $180,000 more than those whose races were characterized as favoring the incumbent, and $270,000 more than those in which the incumbent was considered safe.

Few challengers are able to capitalize on the pitch that their races offer donors a unique opportunity to defeat a powerful incumbent. Only those who mount campaigns against a congressional party leader are able to raise additional large individual contributions, reflecting the leader's unpopularity with donors who support the challenger's party. Challengers also raise less money when facing an incumbent who has strong liberal or conservative leanings.

Republican Anne Northup of Kentucky, who ran as a challenger in 1996, provides an instructive example of how challengers can maximize just a few assets to raise large individual donations. Northup had previous experience as an elected offical, serving in the Kentucky House of Representatives from 1986 to 1996. She also ran in a race that was forecast as extremely competitive against a vulnerable first-term incumbent, Mike Ward. These factors appear to have been instrumental in Northup's ability to raise more than $602,000 in large individual donations. Northup's efforts even far surpassed those of incumbent Ward, who was able to raise $452,000 from PACs, but just $235,000 in large individual donations. By the end of the election, Northup outraised and outspent Ward $1.1 million to $880,000, and won the election by just 1,299 votes.

Few factors influence open-seat candidates' fundraising success in the general election, but competition is one of them. Candidates in 1996 House races where there was no clear frontrunner raised approximately $53,000 more in large individual contributions than did candidates whose races were classified as leaning, $106,000 more than those in which one candidate was favored, and $159,000 more than a candidate who ran for a seat that was classified as safe for one party (see table 5.9). Elected officials raised almost $104,000 more than amateurs. They were clearly able to draw on donors who supported their previous campaigns when running for the House. Candidates whose opponents were unelected politicians raised substantially more than those who were amateurs or elected officials. This fundraising pattern probably reflects the fact that unelected

TABLE 5.9. THE EFFECTS OF COMPETITION-RELATED FACTORS,
PARTISAN INFLUENCES, OCCUPATION, AND DEMOGRAPHIC FACTORS ON
LARGE INDIVIDUAL CONTRIBUTIONS TO HOUSE GENERAL ELECTION
CANDIDATES FOR OPEN SEATS

	Coefficient	*Standard Error*
Competition-Related Factors:		
Elected official	103.52***	33.29
Unelected politician	44.21	40.26
Opponent has held an elected office	−19.01	31.60
Opponent is an unelected politician	86.07**	43.20
Expected competitiveness	53.27***	14.25
Partisan Influences:		
Democrat	−23.92	31.29
Occupation:		
Business	44.65	49.55
Lawyer	87.89**	39.94
Other white-collar professional	130.33*	45.26
Demographic Factors:		
Female	−20.31	43.66
Minority	−85.35**	53.88
Constant	−3.12	
Adj. R-square	.20	
(N)	(108)	

Note: Estimates are based on OLS regression analysis. Figures consist of individual contributions of $200 or more in the 1996 general elections (expressed in $1,000s). See tables 5.7 and 5.8 for variable definitions.
*p<.10, **p<.05, ***p<.01.
Source: The Federal Election Commission.

politicians pose greater challenges to their opponents than do amateurs but are not so formidable as elected officials, who may discourage donors from contributing to their opponents. Those in virtually all occupations raise more money from individuals than do open-seat candidates who work for the armed forces, in agriculture, or in a blue-collar job. Minority candidates also raise substantially less than whites.

Fundraising by Senate Candidates

Senate and House elections differ in many ways, including some aspects of how they are financed.[8] Senate elections are more visible; they generate more earned and paid media than House races. Senate candidates also are more readily recognized by voters. This is especially the case for Senate challengers, whose greater political experience and skills propel them into the spotlight in ways that make most House challengers envious. With the exception of campaigns in the few states that have at-large representation in the House, Senate campaigns must reach larger and more heterogeneous constituencies than House campaigns. Senate campaigns also require greater organization, professional consulting talent, and money. Senate campaigns are more competitive, both in terms of winning votes and collecting campaign dollars, than are House contests (Westle 1991; Abramowitz and Segal 1992; Kahn and Kenney 1997, 1999). Despite the differences between campaigns for the upper and lower chambers, some of the same factors that influence House candidates' abilities to raise large individual contributions also have an impact on Senate candidates' fundraising. Senate incumbents who face well-financed challengers raise more money than those who do not. Expected electoral competition is the strongest predictor of individual receipts for all Senate candidates. It is the most significant factor for challengers and open-seat candidates.

SUMMARY

An individual donor's decision to contribute is influenced by the interaction between the donor's motives and the assets and liabilities of the candidate. Donors' contributions also are influenced by partisanship and ideology, and electoral competitiveness. Perhaps more important, the dynamics of campaign finance are overwhelmingly local: most donors contribute to candidates who represent their district or state.

Investors, unlike other donors, contribute to legislators who serve on committees that can further the donor's business interests. Ideologues donate to candidates in competitive races who belong to the same party or share their ideology. Intimates favor candidates they know, which explains their preference for candidates who belong to the same party, share their ideological beliefs, and run in their home state or congressional district.

Incumbents, challengers, and open-seat candidates raise different amounts from significant donors. Among House incumbents, it is Republicans, party leaders, and first-term members who raise the most. Among challengers and open-seat candidates, previous political experience and expected competitiveness are important. Challengers who run against party leaders also raise more funds, presumably because partisan significant donors view leaders of the opposing party as attractive targets.

These results confirm that although donors are clearly an elite group, they contribute to different candidates to try to accomplish different goals. Nevertheless, despite diversity in their motives and decision rules, their contributions flow primarily to incumbents, reinforcing the incumbent bias in the political system. In this sense, significant donors are not much different from political parties, PACs, and individuals who make small contributions.

chapter 6

The Donors Contact Congress

Significant congressional donors not only contribute money, many also use other methods, such as contacting members of Congress, to further their political goals. In many cases, a contribution makes it easier for a donor, such as a lobbyist, to gain access to an elected official. Alternatively, the contact may precede the contribution; an individual who has been helped by a legislator may be more willing to help the member win reelection. Finally, a contributor may give without any intention of making a personal request of the candidate and without any expectation of contacting the candidate. However, a contribution could lead to an unforeseen contact, as when an issue the donor cares about becomes part of Congress's agenda or the donor needs help from the federal government. A constituent who has made a contribution to a legislator is likely to turn to that individual for help because of the relationship established by the contribution.

The relationship between a contributor and a candidate may begin in any of these ways, but it is often a long-term relationship, sometimes lasting decades. These relationships may evolve over time and become more personal. From most candidates' perspectives, a contribution is the culmination of a courtship with an individual donor. From many donors' points of view, the contact is what consummates the deal. The previous chapters have demonstrated that significant donors have varied reasons for giving, and candidates, in turn, appeal to donors' motives through crafted and targeted solicitations.

This chapter considers an important question: How frequently do donors contact legislators and what are their objectives? Investors and ideologues have policy motives that make them likely to contact members of Congress about legislation. Investors seek to influence legislation that affects their particular business or professional interests, whereas ideologues have broad policy concerns or strong feelings about one or a few controversial issues. An investor who owns a paper company, for example, might contact a member of Congress to express support for a trade bill, such as the North American Free Trade Agreement (NAFTA) because of anticipated profits from reduced foreign tariffs. An ideologue, by comparison, might contact a member of Congress to express opposition to a particular free-trade bill because of environmental, labor, or human-rights concerns.

Intimates, on the other hand, belong to social networks and are typically not interested in obtaining specific benefits for their political activities, including making campaign contributions or visiting with lawmakers. Intimates value personal relationships: they support their friends and are attracted to celebrity politicians, such as those who wield power in Congress (West and Orman 2003). These donors contact politicians for personal reasons.

The purpose of this chapter is to examine the relationships between campaign contributions and contacting members of Congress. We begin by considering how frequently donors contact members of Congress compared to the public, and then we provide an overview of the different reasons donors have for getting in touch with their federal representatives. We conclude by examining the methods significant donors use to influence the legislative process.

CONTACTING CONGRESS

The right to petition the government is enshrined in the U.S. Constitution and a central part of the nation's political ethos. It is as central to Americans' notions of democracy as are the rights to vote, speak freely, and assemble peaceably. Congress, because it is the only directly elected branch of the federal government, is a major focus for representation and lobbying activity.

Indeed, contacting a public official is one of the most common political activities among citizens. Citizens are more likely to contact a public official than participate in any other political act, with the exception of voting (Verba et al. 1995). Citizens contact members of Congress because they want something. Some citizens request information, want to express an opinion, or call on Congress to arrange a tour of the White House, Supreme Court, or U.S. Capitol. Some contacts concern such matters as specific elements of the tax code, regulatory measures, appeals for intervention with a federal agency, or government appropriations for special projects. Some citizen-initiated contacts originate with the individuals themselves. Others are orchestrated by organized groups, such as the NRA (representing gun owners), the Sierra Club (representing environmentalists), or groups on either side of the abortion rights debate (Fowler and Shaiko 1987; Patterson 1999; Cantor 1999).

Some members of the public contact only their own U.S. representative or senators; others target legislators who hold positions of power; still others seem to indiscriminately deluge the institution with postcards, letters, telephone calls, or emails. Political humorist P.J. O'Rourke described one constituent who wrote his congressman every week claiming that the CIA was using low-level microwave radiation to read his thoughts. The congressman, in turn, responded to the letter by suggesting to his constituent that he line his hat with tinfoil (1990).

Of course, members of Congress are not totally without blame if they and their staffs feel overwhelmed with all of this correspondence. Many send questionnaires designed to prompt constituent responses, create relationships of correspondence, and cultivate voter support. Members of Congress also use franked mail, newsletters, Web sites, town-hall meetings, and other communication methods (Adler, Gent, and Overmeyer 1998). Indeed, good communication is an essential part of home style (Fenno 1978). Still, while contacting federal lawmakers is common when compared to other political acts, only a minority of citizens engage in the activity. In 1996, just 12 percent of the public reported any type of contact with a member of Congress over the past year.[1]

Donors are far more willing than the average citizen to contact national lawmakers. Three out of four significant donors reported that they had contacted at least one representative or senator during the past two years. Fully 71 percent reported contacting at least one representative, and nearly two-thirds reported contacting at least one senator (see Figure 6.1). In addition, more than half of all contributors contacted more than one senator or representative, and some 12 percent contacted six or more senators or six or more representatives.

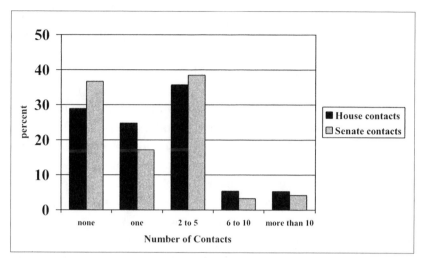

FIGURE 6.1 THE NUMBER OF CONTACTS BY SIGNIFICANT DONORS
Source: The Congressional Donors Survey.

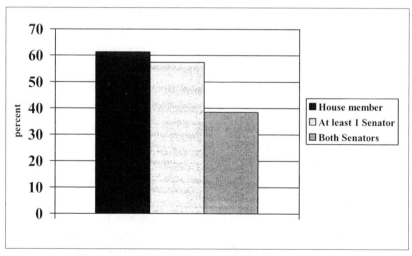

FIGURE 6.2 THE PERCENTAGE OF DONORS WHO CONTACT THEIR OWN
HOUSE MEMBERS AND SENATORS
Source: The Congressional Donors Survey.

One donor, who made many contacts, offered the following reflection, "I often participate in the legislative process. It's kind of like a wave hitting the beach. Any given particle of water does very little, but taken together they really move the sand." Clearly, members of Congress hear the voices of significant donors much more frequently than those of the general public.

Donors most commonly contact their own House member (see figure 6.2). A majority also have contacted one or both senators, with 38 percent having contacted both. These figures reflect the efforts of legislators to build relationships based on trust with their constituents. Members work diligently to convey their qualifications, a sense of identification, and empathy with their constituents. Such relationships are especially important for local donors, many of whom are among the members' strongest supporters, sometimes referred to as their primary constituency (Fenno 1978). From the donors' point of view, contacting their own lawmakers makes sense because they are *their* elected representatives. Committee chairmen and party leaders may control most of the substance of legislation and whether a bill is ever debated in the House or the Senate, but for most donors having their voice heard in Congress begins with their own representative.

Furthermore, these contacts are not the typical correspondence between a constituent and a legislator. In most instances, constituents who contact legislators do not know the member of Congress or senator personally. In contrast, 72 percent of the donors who contacted their House members report being personally acquainted with the member. Indeed, even 36 percent of those individuals who did not contact their House member also were personally acquainted. Almost one-half of all contributors know at least one of their senators personally and 22 percent know both. Members know their key constituents and these people know their members. Just as important, the congressional aides who open the mail are aware of these relationships. They either forward the mail directly to the member (sometimes because it is marked personal or confidential) or they direct the mail to the congressional aide who is best equipped to address the donor's concern.

Although the overwhelming number of contacts is with the donor's own representative or senator, 12 percent of all donors report contacting a legislator from another state. Critics who are concerned about the influence of money in politics emphasize the potential for money to buy influence beyond one's own constituency. It is the local constituency connection, however, that dominates most contacts.

Reasons for Contact

There are several possible reasons that donors initiate contact with a member of Congress. Like other citizens, some donors get in touch with a member to express an opinion or seek information on a bill or policy. Donors also may contact a legislator to seek help for themselves, a family member, or someone they know. Others reach out for social or business reasons. Most congressional aides devote a significant portion of their day to addressing such communications, whether made in the form of mail, email, a telephone call, or a personal visit.

What are the most common reasons that donors get in touch with members of Congress? Roughly half of all significant donors expressed an opinion on a bill (see figure 6.3). About two-fifths also expressed an opinion on a policy, while slightly less than one-fifth sought information on a policy or bill. The nature of each of these contacts relates to legislation, suggesting that donors have broad policy concerns. By comparison, a much smaller percentage of donors—7 and 11 percent, respectively—contacted members of Congress to request help for themselves, a family member, or someone else that they know.

Almost half of all donors contacted a legislator at least once on a matter relating to their job or business. One investor described contacting as an ongoing relationship. "Political influence is generally misunderstood. It

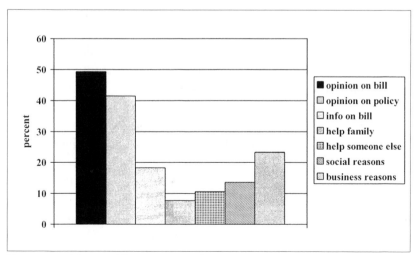

FIGURE 6.3 DONORS' REASONS FOR CONTACTING MEMBERS OF CONGRESS
Source: The Congressional Donors Survey.

is like a conversation: you have to be a part of it to be listened to and some-times you can have an impact on the other participants. Money is a valu-able resource in this conversation, but it is not the most important by any means. A good argument will trump money anytime; a good argument and money is even better."

Significant donors also contact members of Congress for social reasons. As one donor explained, "I talk to hundreds of people a year in every kind of setting. . . I probably see these people as often socially as I do profession-ally. Political types hang out together and not with 'civilians.'" Regardless of their motives, donors call on their representatives at higher rates than the public, and this further amplifies their voice in the political process.

Who Contacts Congress Most Often?

Most donors contact at least one member of Congress, but some commu-nicate with many. Which donors get in touch with the most members of the House and Senate? Habitual donors, individuals who belong to a vari-ety of political organizations, those who solicit contributions for congres-sional candidates, those who are closely attuned to committee politics, and those who are younger and more affluent communicate with more House members than do others (see table 6.1). The same individuals also contact more members of the Senate, as do ideologues. For example, a habitual donor who belongs to eight or more types of groups, who monitors con-gressional politics at the committee level, and who asks others to con-tribute to congressional candidates is 36 percent more likely to contact six or more members of the House and is 22 percent more likely to contact six or more senators than an occasional donor who belongs to one or no groups and who does not help congressional candidates raise money or keep track of committee politics.[2]

Individuals who contact members of Congress are deeply integrated into political networks. Many of the groups to which they belong encour-age their members to write and call members of Congress several times a year. The Sierra Club, the National Realtors Association, and the Nation-al Beer Wholesalers Association, for example, encourage their members to become amateur lobbyists. They provide talking points and introductions to the donors' members of the House and Senate.

Habitual donors and donors who ask others to give to congressional candidates requently come into contact with members of Congress. This

TABLE 6.1. THE EFFECTS OF SIGNIFICANT DONORS' MOTIVES,
CONTRIBUTIONS, POLITICAL INTEGRATION, AND DEMOGRAPHICS ON
THEIR CONTACTS WITH MEMBERS OF CONGRESS

	House	*Senate*
Material motives	.056	.021
	(.041)	(.042)
Purposive motives	.013	.074[*]
	(.041)	(.043)
Solidary motives	.015	.026
	(.041)	(.041)
Habitual donor	.460[***]	.364[***]
	(.085)	(.087)
Membership in number of types of groups	.082[***]	.085[***]
	(.017)	(.018)
Asked others to give	.490[***]	.179[*]
	(.085)	(.088)
Political job	.075	.098
	(.096)	(.098)
Strong partisan	.042	.150
	(.094)	(.096)
Democratic partisanship	−.034	.004
	(.022)	(.022)
Donor follows congressional committee	.596[***]	.406[***]
	(.092)	(.093)
Education	.018	.024
	(.032)	(.033)
Income	.070[*]	.100[**]
	(.041)	(.042)
Refused income	.098	.141
	(.207)	(.216)
Age	−.007[*]	−.007[*]
	(.003)	(.003)
Cut 1	.734	.895
Cut 2	1.557	1.419
Cut 3	2.924	2.884
Cut 4	3.353	3.226
Log Likelihood	−982.40[***]	−929.19[***]
(N)	(783)	(765)

(continued on next page)

(continued from previous page)

Note: Estimates are based on ordered probit regression analysis. Standard errors are in parentheses. The dependent variable is based on the answer to the following question: "During the past two years, how many members of the U.S. House of Representatives, U.S. Senate, or their staffs have you contacted?." Respondents selected from the following choices: 1 = None, 2 = One, 3 = Two to five, 4 = Six to ten, and 5 = more than ten. "Donor follows congressional committee" is a dummy measure that designates whether the donor closely follows the activities of any particular House or Senate congressional committee. See table 4.1 for a definition of the remaining variables.
* p<.05, ** p<.01, *** p<.001.
Source: The Congressional Donors Survey.

contact creates plenty of informal opportunities for them to speak with members. It results in a comfort level which makes it easier for donors to communicate with legislators and their aides. Finally, it is noteworthy that the most affluent donors contact members of Congress most often, further adding to their influence in the political system.

WHY CONTACT MY MEMBER OR YOURS?

Donors not only have a variety of reasons for contacting members of Congress, they may have quite different reasons for contacting members from their district (or state) than members who do not formally represent them. Donor motives have a major impact on which politicians they contact and why. As noted above, virtually all donors contact their own member, but their level of political sophistication and specific motives may result in their targeting appeals to other legislators who can help donors achieve various goals. For example, members from out of state can often provide specific information, may have the clout to move specific pieces of legislation through Congress, or may invite them to a fundraising event where Barbra Streisand, Charlton Heston, or some other luminary is in attendance. In some cases, all of these reasons are important. As one donor explained, "I really do it all: I write, I talk, I testify, and I meet these guys socially. Some of my contacts deal with [my] business and others deal with other people's business. . . . Donors are usually disappointed when all their check gets them is access. But they soon realize access is better than no access, and getting to talk to someone about their problems is very therapeutic."

In-District or In-State Contacts

As has been pointed out above, donors contact members of Congress for many reasons. The logistic regression results demonstrate that ideologues are the most likely to contact their members of Congress on a bill (see table 6.2, column 1).[3] They are 14 percent more likely to do this if their member shares their ideology, and 9 percent more like to do so if the two of them belong to the same party.[4] This also holds true for expressing an opinion about a specific policy (see table 6.2, column 2). Donors who follow the details of policymaking at the committee level are 9 percent more likely to express opinions about a policy or seek information about a bill.

Investors contact their House member and senators to seek information about a bill or policy 6 percent more often than do other donors (see table 6.2, column 3). Donors who share their members' party affiliation and are attuned to the nuances of the legislative process, particularly at the committee level, are very strongly inclined to seek information from their legislators. They use this information to assess how congressional action—or inaction—may affect their business.

Not surprisingly, those who are motivated by material concerns are much more likely than other donors to call on their federal lawmakers for business reasons (see table 6.2, column 4). Investors are 28 percent more likely to get in touch with a member of the House about a business-related issue than are others.[5] Partisanship and ideology condition their propensity to make these contacts. Members of the same party and donors with the same basic political philosophy are much more likely to contact their member for business reasons, as are independents. Only members of the opposing party appear somewhat disinclined to contact their representatives for business purposes. Wealthier donors are also more likely to contact their members.

Investors are only slightly more likely than other types of donors to turn to their members for help for themselves or their families (see table 6.2, column 5). Intimates are 4 percent more likely to call on their member to help others (see table 6.2, column 6). This contact is more likely to be the case when wealthy donors share their members' party affiliation and ideology. Intimates become involved in politics because they enjoy personal relationships. As a result of their involvement in political and social networks they are more likely to be approached by friends for help and to have the personal connections with their members of Congress to get results.

TABLE 6.2. REASONS FOR CONTACTING ONE'S OWN MEMBER OF CONGRESS

	Opinion bill	Opinion policy	Info Bill/ policy	Business reasons	Help you or family	Help someone else	Social reasons
Material motives	-.064	-.088	.199**	.724***	.215*	-.083	-.080
Purposive motives	.331***	.323***	.122	.067	-.165	.088	.310*
Solidary motives	-.130*	-.136*	.013	-.045	.036	.308**	.335***
Party agreement	.359*	.514**	.685**	.583**	.207	1.167**	.960**
Political independent	.067	.190	-.148	.475*	-.341	.734	1.123**
Ideological similarity	.107*	.138**	.106	-.053	.408**	.282*	.182
Senate candidate	.307*	.236	.315	.212	-.262	-.050	-.262
Senate candidate not up for reelection	-.587***	-.523***	-.580**	-.612**	-.480	-.560*	-.692*
Donor follows congressional committee	.170	.388***	.534**	.234	.318	-.360	.166
Candidate is member of committee that donor follows	-.033	.357	.313	.131	-.288	.493	.450
Habitual donor	.156	.218*	.216	.016	.005	.150	.170
Income	.035	-.056	.041	.173*	-.101	.211*	.326**
Refused income	-.133	-.864**	.125	-.541	-1.554	1.027	-.199
Constant	-1.106	-1.476	-3.210	-2.204	-4.697	-5.628	-5.264
(N)	(1,366)	(1,366)	(1,366)	(1,366)	(1,366)	(1,366)	(1,366)

Note: Estimates are based on logistic regression analysis. See table 5.3 for a definition of the variables. See also table 4.1 for a definition of material, purposive, and solidary motives.

* p<.05, ** p<.01, *** p<.001.

Source: The Congressional Donors Survey.

By definition, intimates should be more likely to contact their members for social reasons (see table 6.2, column 7). Not surprisingly, they are. As one intimate explained, "I rarely contact members of Congress . . . with the exception of my own congressman, who is a long-time friend. . . . I don't keep track of Congress much at all."

However, partisanship is also important. Donors feel most comfortable socializing with members of their own party. Independents also enjoy social contacts with members of both parties. Donors from an opposing party, however, rarely feel comfortable socializing with their member. Wealthier donors, who move in the same circles as members of Congress, are more likely to call upon them for social occasions.

Out-of-District or Out-of-State Contacts

Members of Congress who do not formally represent voters in a certain state or district are not on those voters' immediate radar screen, and donors very rarely contact a legislator who does not formally represent them. The odds of any significant donor contacting a particular member of Congress from outside of their district or state are extremely low. Of the 304,308 possible pairings of donors and members of Congress from outside a donor's district or state, only 328 resulted in contacts—just 0.1 percent. Nevertheless, there are reasons why congressional donors may want to contact a legislator of the House or Senate who does not formally represent them. Investors sometimes need to communicate with a committee chair in order to make their views on a specific bill heard early in the legislative process. Ideologues may feel their views are better represented by a representative or senator from another state, particularly if their own legislators belong to the opposing party. Some intimates, particularly those who are affluent, may combine a business or personal trip with attendance at a fundraiser in the nation's capital, New York City, Chicago, or some other city that offers a variety of amenities.

The results of rare-events logit analysis demonstrate that regardless of their motives, donors are more likely to contact a legislator who does not formally represent them to express an opinion about a bill or policy if that member shares their ideology and does not belong to the opposing party (see table 6.3, columns 1 and 2).[6] For example, donors are almost six times more likely to contact such a member to express an opinion on a specific policy if that member shares their ideology. As one donor noted, "Over the

TABLE 6.3. REASONS FOR CONTACTING MEMBER OF CONGRESS OUTSIDE DISTRICT

	Opinion bill	Opinion policy	Info Bill/policy	Business reasons	Help someone else	Social reasons
Material motives	.056	.086	.322**	.529***	.341*	-.036
Purposive motives	-.109	-.128	-.261*	-.217*	.035	-.174
Solidary motives	.049	-.054	-.040	-.031	-.057	.210*
Party agreement	.722**	.672**	.562	.203	1.589**	1.304**
Political independent	.870***	.629*	.279	.607*	1.170	.948
Ideological similarity	.262***	.311**	.224	.324**	.514**	.195
Senate	.334	.465	-.500	.157	1.295*	1.378***
Senate candidate not up for reelection	-.225	-.322	.552	.052	-1.416	-.713
Donor follows congressional committee	.644***	.902***	1.399***	.610**	-.525	.759**
Candidate is member of committee that donor follows	1.025***	1.184***	.200	1.156***	1.288*	1.461***
Habitual donor	-.147	-.048	.098	-.336	-.112	-.823***
Income	.040	.093	-.168	-.043	.130	.306**
Refused income	.486	.787*	-.274	-.069	1.662*	.458
Constant	-9.511	-10.347	-10.020	-9.852	-13.406	-11.452
(N)	(256,798)	(256,798)	(256,798)	(256,798)	(256,798)	(256,798)

Note: Estimates are based on rare-events logit analysis. There were too few contacts made to help the donor or a family member of a member of Congress outside the district to run the full model. See table 5.3 for a definition of the variables. See also table 4.1 for a definition of material, purposive, and solidary motives.
* p<.05, ** p<.01, *** p<.001.
Source: The Congressional Donors Survey.

years, I have cultivated contacts with about four dozen candidates. They all share my basic politics. . . . I rarely back liberals, and so I rarely talk to them." As was the case for in-district or in-state contacts, having the political sophistication to follow particular congressional committees is an important factor. Out-of-district-contacts are more narrowly focused: donors are roughly three times more likely to contact legislators who serve on committees they follow closely.

Investors are more likely than other donors, particularly ideologues, to contact a member from outside their district or state to gain information about a bill or policy (see table 6.3, column 3). As one investor explained, "One reason I support members of Congress is so they will keep me informed. . . . It is part of their job." Those who follow specific committees are four times as likely as other donors to communicate with a member who does not come from their state or district for political information. As one donor described this process, "I contact many members of Congress every year. . . . I follow the Ways and Means Committee and the Small Business committee."

As one would expect, investors are four times more likely than others to contact lawmakers who do not formally represent them for business reasons (see table 6.3, column 4). Ideologues were the least likely to get in touch with members of Congress for business reasons. Donors are six times more likely to contact members who share their pro-business ideology, and they are three times more likely to communicate with members who serve on a committee these donors follow closely. Most investors are pragmatic and access-oriented, seek particularistic benefits for their business or industry, and recognize that these benefits are generally inserted into legislation when it is at the committee or subcommittee level.

What about when donors ask for help for themselves or others? It is so rare for donors to seek help for themselves or a family member from a member of Congress who does not formally represent them that it is impossible to make generalizations about who does this and why. This stands in sharp contrast to the in-district contacts described above. Donors direct problems related to constituency service and casework to their own representatives; problems related to someone else's business matters are raised with members of Congress who have the interest and power to intercede (see table 6.3, column 5). Donors are more likely to ask for help from legislators who belong to their party or who serve on a committee they follow. Ideology has an especially big impact. Donors who share the same ideology as a member of Congress are 24 times more likely to ask that member for help than a member who holds the opposing political philosophy.

Intimates are almost twice as likely as others to have social contact with national legislators other than their own members of the House and Senate (see table 6.3, column 6).[7] They are four times more likely to want to socialize with legislators who share their party affiliation. Surprisingly, these social contacts are more common with members who serve on committees which the members follow closely. It may be that the relationships they forge with these out-of state legislators lead to friendships that last beyond debates over individual pieces of legislation.

INFLUENCING AN ACT OF CONGRESS

While congressional donors and everyday citizens contact members of Congress for many reasons, they also make concrete attempts to influence acts of Congress. Indeed, donors use a variety of approaches to influence the legislative process, and many use more than one. Fully 81 percent of contributors have at least once in their lives attempted to do so. These policy-oriented contacts can take many forms. Nearly three out of four significant donors wrote letters to members of Congress; this type of effort was common even among those who knew their legislator personally and among those who worked as lobbyists. Almost 70 percent talked to a legislator or congressional aide about a piece of legislation. Nearly 50 percent worked through some kind of formal group, another 34 percent worked through a political party, and 23 percent worked through an informal group. A remarkable 14 percent have testified before Congress (see figure 6.4). Given that testifying before Congress is a luxury that few citizens get to enjoy, the latter percentage speaks volumes about the political clout of significant congressional donors.

Those with different motives use different methods to try to influence legislation. Investors with strong material motives speak personally with members or their staff or work through formal groups (such as PACs), and they are especially unlikely to work through political parties (see table 6.4). For example, investors are 14 percent more likely to have spoken to a member and are 11 percent more likely to have spoken to a congressional aide than are donors who do not contribute for material reasons.[8] Those

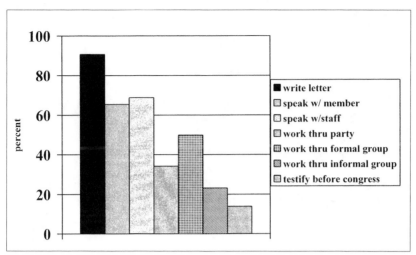

FIGURE 6.4 METHODS USED TO INFLUENCE AN ACT OF CONGRESS
Source: The Congressional Donors Survey.

who seek particularistic benefits from government primarily speak directly to those who can influence policy. One donor put it this way:

> If you have never started a new business and tried to grow it, you
> have no idea of the number of government hoops that must be
> jumped. It is often necessary to obtain the assistance of a politician's
> constituent service staff simply to move routine paperwork from one
> agency to another. That staff is usually more responsive to those who
> are significant contributors and will move their matters to the head of
> their to-do list.

Those who pursue purposive goals are more likely to use all forms of
contacting except testifying before Congress. Ideologues are especially
distinctive, however, in the frequency with which they write letters to
members of Congress. They are, on average, about 12 percent more likely to contact a member using any of these means. Intimates, by contrast,
are 14 percent more likely to work through a political party than are other donors.[9]

Attentiveness to congressional committees and group membership
also have a major impact on how significant donors get in touch with Congress. Donors who belong to eight or more groups, for example, are at
least 20 percent more likely to write a member of Congress, speak with a

	Written to member of Congress	Spoken with member	Spoken with staff	Worked through party	Worked formal group	Worked informal group	Testified before Congress
Material motives	.087	.226**	.188**	-.087	.206**	.079	.212*
Purposive motives	.370***	.140*	.290***	.368***	.296***	.300**	.112
Solidary motives	-.113	.080	.080	.319***	1.02	.247**	.270**
Habitual donor	.119	.668***	.751***	.105	.246	.243	.389
Membership in number of types of groups	.224***	.212***	.152***	.199***	.180***	.061	.152**
Asked others to give	.511**	.873***	.745**	.661***	.143	.652**	.239
Political job	.007	.021	.158	.179	.101	-.033	-.086
Strong partisan	-.195	-.167	.075	.856***	.508**	.081	.297
Democratic partisanship	-.055	-.020	-.029	-.007	.174***	.124**	-.019
Donor follows congressional committee	.789***	1.154***	.895***	.418*	.854***	.943***	1.490***
Education	.261***	.089	-.053	.025	.205***	.046	.227*
Income	-.043	.098	.064	-.089	.221*	.169*	.079
Refused income	-.398	-.139	.133	-.454	.275	.428	-.354
Age	.012*	.009	-.009	.003	.004	.010	.043***
Constant	-2.611	-4.317	-1.920	-3.183	-4.736	-5.522	-9.030
(N)	(795)	(795)	(795)	(795)	(795)	(795)	(795)

Note: Estimates are based on logistic regression analysis. See table 4.1 for variable definitions.

* p<.05, ** p<.01, *** p<.001.

Source: The Congressional Donors Survey.

congressional aide, or work through a party or a formal group than are those who belong to one or no organizations. Moreover, donors who belong to this many groups are 30 percent more likely to speak with a member of Congress than are others.[10] This pattern reflects the efforts that political organizations make to get their members to reach out to members of Congress, especially when legislation of importance to the group is under consideration (see, e.g., Fowler and Shaiko 1987).

Finally, partisanship matters: strong partisans are 18 percent more likely to try to influence policy making through their party and 12 percent more likely to work through a formal group than are other donors. Democratic donors are more likely to work through formal and informal groups than are Republicans. Donors' motives, political awareness, and political integration are thus closely connected to the methods that they use to influence legislation.

SUMMARY

Donors engage in many forms of political activity. They seek to influence the political process before, during, and after elections. Campaign contributions constitute one important route of influence. Directly contacting members of Congress and their aides constitutes another. Unlike most citizens, an overwhelming majority of significant donors know their member of Congress and communicate with them personally. Most donors get in touch with a member to express an opinion or seek information on a bill or policy, but many make contact for business or social reasons or to seek help for themselves, a family member, or someone they know.

More important, for many donors it is clear that contacting serves as a useful supplement to giving as a way to influence the political process. Most donors follow up their contribution with some form of communication, or they make contacts first and then follow up with contributions. Donors are strategic when they reach out to members of Congress. They get in touch with their own representatives for casework, and they get in touch with members on key committees who do not formally represent them for assistance with their business interests.

chapter 7

Congressional Donors and Campaign Reform

Congressional donors are involved in a campaign finance system that has been sharply criticized by political commentators, academics, and current and former members of Congress. Although most donors willingly participate in the system, this does not mean they support it. The missing element in the story of the campaign finance system is the opinions of the donors themselves. How do donors evaluate the system, and what are their views on campaign finance reform? How are they likely to respond to the recently enacted Bipartisan Campaign Reform Act of 2002?

Significant donors' opinions are important for several reasons. First, they constitute a major source of the money spent in congressional elections. If these donors become sufficiently disenchanted with the campaign finance system, they might withdraw from it. Second, they experience the campaign finance system from a very different perspective than do the public, the candidates, the media, and the political consultants who make a living raising money. Donors are better informed about election campaigns and the fundraising process than is the general public. Third, because they are active participants in the system, legislators who would further reform the campaign finance system are likely to anticipate their reactions.

DONORS AND THE CAMPAIGN FINANCE SYSTEM

Congressional contributors have personal knowledge of how the campaign finance system actually works, and their assessments of the system are quite revealing. When asked about the campaign finance system, 85 percent of all significant donors agreed with the statement, "contributing is a legitimate form of participation" (see table 7.1). This should not be surprising because every member of the donor pool has actually made a contribution. Nevertheless, 5 percent disagreed.

Some donors defended their right to make contributions with a tone of defiance. As one donor commented:

> If I earn enough money to give to candidates, why should there be laws preventing it? . . . The biggest problem is they are trying to level off the playing field. They are taking away our rights as Americans.

This donor clearly believes that liberty is more important than equality in American democracy. He embraces the notion that citizens with more money ought to have a greater influence in politics in a capitalist system.

Other donors acknowledged that campaign contributions could create the appearance of impropriety. As one donor stated, "Giving money to a candidate one supports is valid. But there is a danger that people will assume that politicians are being 'bought.'" Occurrences of bribery are rare, but the perception among the public is that it is common.[1]

TABLE 7.1. SIGNIFICANT DONORS' ATTITUDES TOWARD THE
CAMPAIGN FINANCE SYSTEM

	Agree	*No Opinion*	*Disagree*
Contributing is a legitimate form of participation	85%	10	5
Officeholders regularly pressure donors for money	80%	12	8
Donors regularly pressure officials for favors	57%	23	19
Money is the single most important factor in elections	55%	16	29
Most donors are motivated by ideology	54%	26	19
Most donors are seeking access to government	53%	22	24
(N)	(1,029)	(1,029)	(1,029)

Note: Some rows do not add up to 100 percent due to rounding.
Source: The Congressional Donors Survey.

Many donors believe in the legitimacy of campaign contributions but are troubled by certain aspects of the role of money in politics. In fact, many are ambivalent about making campaign contributions. One congressional donor noted:

> Giving money is just something that has to be done. . . . People will try to influence the government as long as it influences their businesses and lives. So there is no real solution.

Numerous donors feel put upon by the incessant solicitations they receive. Fully four-fifths of the significant donors complain that officeholders regularly pressure them for money. One ideologue was particularly vocal on the subject, stating, "The level of fundraising is very problematic. If you are a donor, everyone will hit you up day in and day out. But since politics is necessary, one learns to deal with the pressure to contribute." Another donor remarked, "Fundraising reached ridiculous proportions in the [1996] election and that is where some of the abuses came from. The more pressure there is to give, the more chances someone will make a mistake." One donor who routinely solicits contributions for the candidates he supports was especially candid:

> Candidates do pressure donors, more than the other way around. Hell, I pressure donors. This is because it costs so much to run for office and money is hard to raise. Some people are upset because fundraising and campaigns are now year-round, all the time activities.

Moreover, almost as many donors as citizens believe that donors pressure officials for favors. It is remarkable that people who contribute money to candidates admit that contribution activity is often self-serving. This provides strong evidence for some of the sharpest criticisms of the campaign finance system.

Donors are divided over the role of money in elections. Just over one-half of all significant donors agreed that money is the single most important factor in elections. The high cost of elections was central to this concern and widely understood to be the chief source of the pressure that campaigns place on prospective donors to make contributions. One donor put it this way:

It is so tremendously expensive to run for public office these days. I was in public office for about eight years, thirty-five years ago, and it was relatively inexpensive to run a campaign. We often ask about candidates and how much money they can raise, and the answer is always grim.

Another argued:

The level of spending does irritate people and even worse the level of fundraising is problematic. During a campaign, I am badgered constantly and it really angers me. . . . I wish we could get the costs of campaigns under control.

Donors also were divided in their opinions about why individuals contribute. More than half of the significant donors agreed that most donors are motivated by ideology, a view that is consistent with the prominence of purposive motivations among donors. But almost as many donors agreed that "most donors are seeking access to government." Of course, both these perceptions could have an element of truth (see Morin and Brossard 1997).

Given these opinions, how do donors evaluate the campaign finance system as a whole and the need for reform? Nearly a third of the significant donors believed that the federal campaign finance system was "broken and needs to be replaced," and nearly half agreed that "it has problems and needs to be changed" (see table 7.2). Another fifth felt it has "some problems but is basically sound." Virtually no donors reported the system to be "all right the way it is." Put another way, better than three-quarters of the donors saw major problems with the finance system, and nearly all admitted enough difficulties to warrant change. These findings are consistent with opinions voiced by the general public, the nation's business executives, and congressional candidates.[2] Indeed, roughly three times as many donors and candidates characterized the system as broken than did the general public, although the public was more likely to claim the system had problems, and a slightly smaller portion of the public reported positive views.

It is striking that donors who make significant contributions to congressional candidates, as well as other types of candidates, party committees, and PACs are so critical of the campaign finance system. As one contributor argued:

TABLE 7.2. SIGNIFICANT DONORS', CONGRESSIONAL CANDIDATES', AND
THE PUBLIC'S ASSESSMENTS OF THE CAMPAIGN FINANCE SYSTEM

	Significant Donors	*General Public*	*Congressional Candidates*
It is broken and needs to be replaced	32%	12%	40%
It has problems and needs to be changed	46	70	39
It has some problems but is basically sound	21	14	21
It is all right just the way it is and should not be changed	2	4	1
(N)	(1,027)	(807)	(326)

Note: Congressional candidates include major-party primary and general-election candidates who ran in 2000. Some columns do not add up to 100 percent due to rounding.
Sources: The Congressional Donors Survey; Paul S. Herrnson, The Campaign Assessment and Candidate Outreach Project 2000; *Washington Post* Poll 1/14–1/19, 1997.

> Campaign finance today has polluted the political system of our country. The whole system is increasingly sick and perverse. We need some radical reform; look at the whole system. The system can't be fixed by tinkering. . . . The whole system is corrupt in my opinion.

Another donor offered this reflective comment:

> You need to ask, "Do we really believe in our hearts and in the pits of our stomach that this system is the best we can do, or can we improve it?" I would hope idealistically that the overwhelming response is we can improve it and we have to improve it so we can at least go forward with a kind of consensus that the current system is morally bankrupt. Having said that, I need to say that I participate in that moral bankruptcy on a regular basis, and I almost feel guilty for it. But I don't know another way to do it.

The tension between their dislike of the system and the internal and external reasons they have to give help explain why they participate in a system they so freely criticize. In the short run, many donors believe they have a big stake in politics and that they have few other means of protecting that stake than making donations.

Some also commented about the futility of campaign finance reform. For instance, one donor asserted, "We are very pragmatic people: change the rules and we will adjust. That is because what we do isn't really all that bad." Another went on in somewhat greater detail:

> Critics tend to misunderstand the role of money. Candidates ask for money, they don't "pressure" like your survey suggests. Likewise, donors don't "pressure" either—they just give. Behind all this are personal relationships that make the difference; money just lubricates those relationships, it doesn't create them or destroy them. The problem is that some of these relationships get built into law, and often the law is bad for everyone. Here the liberals are right. Where they are wrong is that many of the bad laws are their own creations.

Donors' values, interests, and experiences color their assessments of the campaign finance system. Factor analysis confirms there are three underlying dimensions to donors' opinions about the campaign finance system.[3] The most prominent is a "pressure-and-access" dimension, which is concerned with candidates pressuring donors, donors pressuring candidates, and contributing to obtain access. A second, "civic-participation" dimension is based on the belief that campaign contributing is a legitimate form of participation and donors give on the basis of ideology. The third dimension might be called "money drives politics." It includes donors' overall evaluations of the campaign finance system as well their belief that money is the most important factor in elections.

Occasional donors are somewhat more likely to believe there is significant pressure for contributions and access than are habitual donors (see table 7.3). They are less likely to maintain that campaign contributions are a legitimate form of civic participation. More than 90 percent of the habitual donors consider campaign contributions a legitimate form of participation; 77 percent of occasional donors hold the same view. Habitual donors also are slightly more likely to believe the campaign finance system is sound. Occasional donors also are more likely to hold the opinion that money drives politics.

The debate over campaign finance has been conducted largely along partisan lines. As one would expect, there are partisan differences in donors' evaluations on all three aspects of the campaign finance system. Democratic and independent donors are more likely to consider the campaign finance system broken: 40 percent of the Democrats and 38

TABLE 7.3. SIGNIFICANT DONORS' EVALUATIONS OF THE CAMPAIGN
FINANCE SYSTEM

	Pressure and Access	*Civic Participation*	*Money Drives Politics*
Level of Giving:			
Occasional	.093	−.178	.130
Habitual	−.090	.172	−.126
F =	8.870**	32.907***	17.483***
Partisanship:			
Democrats	.190	−.047	.126
Republicans	−.166	.091	−.140
Independents	.125	−.178	.168
F =	14.807***	5.733**	10.684***
Motives:			
Investors	.070	−.102	.050
Ideologues	−.086	.131	.015
Intimates	.090	−.020	−.005
Incidentals	.026	−.170	−.067
F =	1.905	4.529**	.434
(N)	(1,047)	(1,047)	(1,047)

Note: Figures represent average factor-solution scores. A high score represents agreement
and a low score represents disagreement with the above positions. Statistical significance
based on ANOVA tests.
* $p < .05.$, ** $p < .01$, *** $p < .001$
Source: The Congressional Donors Study.

percent of the independents hold this view, compared to 25 percent of
the Republicans.

The only significant disagreement among investors, ideologues, intimates, and incidentals concerns the civic participation elements of contributing. Ideologues have the most positive opinion of campaign contributions, perhaps because they make donations to support candidates who
share their values and issue stances. Incidentals are the most critical, followed by investors and intimates. The investors' perspectives probably
reflect their belief that giving is a necessary evil. The intimates' mild pes-
simism is undoubtedly influenced by the fact that for them a campaign
contribution is often little more than the price of admission for a fancy
social event.

Donors' Views on Campaign Finance Reform Proposals

Despite differences in their opinions about the current campaign finance system, significant donors hold similar views on many of the campaign finance reforms that have been recently debated in Congress and the national media. The most popular reform proposal among donors was eliminating large soft-money contributions (see table 7.4). This proposal—the centerpiece of the recently enacted BCRA—was supported by 77 percent of all significant donors. Occasional and habitual donors of both parties shared this sentiment.

Donors' antipathy toward soft money is informed both by their view that it corrupts the political process and that they are continually pressured to give larger amounts. The comments of one donor were typical of donors who favored banning large soft-money donations: "I keep getting frustrated with what's going on with soft money. Big, apparently anony-

TABLE 7.4. SIGNIFICANT DONORS' ATTITUDES TOWARD SPECIFIC CAMPAIGN FINANCE REFORM PROPOSALS

	Agree	*No Opinion*	*Disagree*
Eliminate large soft-money contributions	77%	11	12
Placing a limit on spending by congressional candidates	74%	6	20
Limit TV advertising of congressional candidates	63%	12	25
Ban PACs from giving money to congressional candidates	52%	15	33
Give free media time and postage to candidates	41%	15	45
Provide public funding for congressional candidates	39%	15	46
Allow individuals to make larger gifts to candidates	37%	21	43
Eliminate all limitations and require full disclosure	34%	18	48
Allow parties to make larger gifts to candidates	26%	23	51
(N)	(1,030)	(1,030)	(1,030)

Note: Some rows do not add up to 100 percent due to rounding.
Source: The Congressional Donors Survey.

mous donations are the worst aspect of our system today." One donor added, "I think this soft-money thing is just a way to squeeze more money out of donors. People can't say 'I maxed out' anymore. In my heart, I'd like to see all that eliminated."

Nevertheless, some donors expressed worries about the effects restricting soft money could have on elections. As one contributor remarked, "Without [soft money], Bob Dole would be president and that troubles me. . . . [C]linton would not have been competitive just on public funds and the small money from his supporters."

Placing limits on spending by congressional candidates is also popular, garnering the support of three-fourths of all significant donors and almost as many major donors. Donor support for this reform is only 10 percent lower than that reported for the public, most of whom make no contributions. Contributors argued that limiting candidate spending would "even the playing field" and "reduce the impact of money on election outcomes." Some donors recognized that spending limits could run up against First Amendment protections for the freedom of speech and the Supreme Court's ruling in *Buckley v. Valeo* (1976), but this did not dim their zeal for this reform (Bonifaz, Luke, and Wright 2001).

An indirect way to limit the costs of congressional elections would be to place limits on candidates' access to the public airwaves. Nearly two-thirds of the significant donors backed this provision, despite the fact that it would probably run into the same First Amendment challenges as campaign spending limits. Just over one-half of all significant donors supported a ban on PAC contributions to congressional candidates, which was a staple of reform proposals prior to the growth of soft money in the 1990s (Mutch 1999).

Donors disagree in their support for public subsidies–whether in the form of cash or free media time or postage. Public subsidies are substantially less popular among congressional donors than are attempts to limit the flow of campaign resources. One referred to them as "welfare for politicians." Nevertheless, these reforms had some champions among the donors. Some preferred instituting a matching funds system similar to that used to finance presidential nominations. One contributor advocated enacting public funding systems like those adopted in some of the states:

> If it were up to me, I would prefer a system of public finance, something like Maine has now adopted. It seems to me that giving the two candidates equal resources so that the elections are decid-

ed on the basis of issues rather than how much money each candidate has would be a great improvement of our current system.

The least popular reform proposals embrace different aspects of deregulation: allowing individuals or parties to make larger contributions, or eliminating contribution limits in favor of full disclosure. These approaches have been defended on several grounds: the real value of the hard-money limits have decreased by inflation and rising campaign costs; fully disclosed hard money is preferable to undisclosed soft money; and the regime regulating campaign finance has become so eroded it ought to be done away with altogether (see Smith 2001; Anderson 2000a). None of these approaches is popular with significant donors. Many donors doubtlessly believe that raising contribution limits would both increase the pressure on them to contribute, and increase the influence of others who are willing to give more.

How do donors' attitudes on these disparate reforms fit together? We used factor analysis to measure three underlying dimensions.[4] The most prominent dimension concerns "regulatory reform," including banning large soft-money donations, limiting candidate spending and TV advertising, and abolishing PACs. The second dimension involves "deregulatory reform," such as allowing larger individual and party donations or contribution limits in favor of full disclosure. The final dimension is "public financing," comprising direct monetary subsidies of candidates and media time and postage.

Donor evaluations of the system are an important source of attitudes toward reform. Donors who think the system revolves too much around pressure and access favor regulatory reforms according to the results of our OLS regressions (see table 7.5). Donors who believe contributions are a legitimate form of civic participation, by contrast, prefer a more free-market approach, opposing increased regulation, preferring deregulation, and voicing negative views about public subsidies. Donors who believe money drives politics are the least inclined toward free-market approaches. They favor increased regulation and public subsidies and oppose deregulation.

Partisanship also has a major impact on donors' attitudes toward reform. Democrats are modestly more likely than Republicans and independents to favor increased regulation. Democrats are much more likely to oppose deregulation. Partisan differences are the greatest on public subsidies, reflecting more general party differences on the role of government

TABLE 7.5. SIGNIFICANT DONORS' SUPPORT FOR REGULATORY REFORMS AND PUBLIC SUBSIDIES

	Increased Regulation	Deregulation	Public Subsidies
Pressure and access	.09***	.02	-.01
	(.03)	(.03)	(.03)
Civic participation	-.15***	.14**	-.09***
	(.03)	(.03)	(.03)
Money drives politics	.41***	-.30***	.26***
	(.03)	(.03)	(.03)
Material motives	-.02	.01	-.06*
	(.03)	(.03)	(.03)
Purposive motives	-.01	-.01	.02
	(.03)	(.03)	(.03)
Solidary motives	.01	-.04	.05
	(.03)	(.03)	(.03)
Habitual donor	-.12*	-.08	-.04
	(.06)	(.06)	(.06)
Political job	-.28***	-.12*	-.07
	(.07)	(.07)	(.07)
Woman	-.08	-.01	.04
	(.07)	(.08)	(.07)
Democratic partisanship	.08***	-.14***	.21***
	(.02)	(.02)	(.02)
Education	-.05*	.03	.11***
	(.02)	(.02)	(.02)
Income	-.02	.01	.02
	(.03)	(.03)	(.03)
Refused income	-.22	-.03	-.01
	(.15)	(.16)	(.14)
Age	.01***	-.01	.004*
	(.01)	(.01)	(.002)
Constant	-.41	.51**	-1.4***
	(.20)	(.22)	(.20)
Adj. R-square	.31	.19	.30
(N)	(915)	(915)	(915)

Note: Coefficients are OLS regression estimates. Standard errors are in parentheses. "Pressure and access," "legitimacy of contributions," and "system broken" are factor solutions generated from the donor's responses to a battery of questions about the role of money in politics and their views on campaign finance reform. See table 4.1 for a definition of the remaining variables.
* p <.05, ** p<.01, *** p<.001.
Source: The Congressional Donors Study.

subsidies.[5] The more strongly they identify with the Democratic Party the more intensely they hold these views.

Habitual donors are distinctive only in their opposition to increased regulation. Donors' motives, occupation, and other demographic characteristics do not contribute as consistently to their positions on campaign reform as do the other factors. The investors—with their high material motives—oppose public subsidies, probably reflecting their general free-market orientation. Income and gender have no significant impact on donors' reform preferences. Those with higher levels of education oppose increased regulation and are much more likely to favor public subsidies. Older voters, who remember the Watergate break-in and other campaign finance scandals, are somewhat more inclined toward regulatory measures.

Donors who work in politics are more likely to oppose both increased regulation and deregulation, presumably because many of them are used to working under the current system and have established routines for contributing to and contacting congressional candidates. Some of these donors also may question the constitutionality of some of the proposed reforms. However, many officeholders and political aides are somewhat more likely to support regulation, reflecting the fact that some of them are constantly dunned for money and are routinely exposed to the corrosive effects of the fundraising process and the amount of time it entails (Francia and Herrnson 2001).

Despite donor and citizen support for reform, Congress failed to pass campaign finance reform legislation during the 1990s. A consensus had developed among donors acknowledging that there was a problem, and there was agreement on some solutions, including a ban on soft money. Despite the complaints that many of them had about the campaign finance system, it is unlikely that many of them lobbied heavily on this issue. None were in a position to overcome the intransigence of congressional party leaders, who were sharply divided on the issue.

The Bipartisan Campaign Finance Reform Act

Partisan and ideological differences were significant impediments to passing reform proposals, even where there was a strong consensus across the political spectrum, such as banning large soft-money donations.[6] Only a compromise combining both a ban on large soft-money donations with an increase in individual contribution limits made it possible for BCRA to pass in 2002. No doubt increasingly critical views of the campaign finance system were important to the eventual compromise, allowing key Republicans Senator John McCain of Arizona and Representative Christopher Shays of Connecticut to work with their Democratic counterparts Senator Russell Feingold of Wisconsin and Representative Martin Meehan of Massachusetts to pass the bill (Allen 2002).

The most highly publicized aspects of the BCRA are its outlawing national-party soft money and its restrictions on mass-media advertising by corporations, trade associations, unions, and other groups. However, the law also has provisions that promise to have a direct impact on individual contributors and congressional campaigns. The BCRA allows individuals to contribute $2,000 to candidates in each phase of an election (primary, general, and runoff), doubling the previous legal limit. It also raises the aggregate ceiling for individual contributions to federal candidates to $37,500 per two-year election cycle, and sets at $95,000 the two-year maximum contributions that individuals can contribute to federal candidates, PACs, and national party committees.

The passage of the new law involved considerable debate in both houses of Congress and invoked some passionate exchanges. The bill's Senate sponsors based much of their case on the need to lessen the effects of money in politics and counter public cynicism about government. In McCain's words:

> This legislation will provide much needed reform of our federal election campaign laws. With the stroke of the president's pen, we will eliminate hundreds of millions of dollars of unregulated soft money that has caused Americans to question the integrity of their elected representatives. This is a good bill, it is a legally sound bill, and it is a fair bill that benefits neither party, but that profits our political system and that will, I hope, help to restore the public's faith in government (McCain 2002).

Feingold's argument for the legislation focused more directly on pubic perceptions of the role of money and politics:

Money shouldn't define this democracy, and it doesn't have to. We don't have to pick up the paper and read headlines like *Influence Market: Industries That Backed Bush Are Now Seeking Return on Investment*. That's a headline that ran on March 6th in the *Wall Street Journal*. I think we all know what that means, and so does everyone else. The assumption that we can be bought, or that the President of the United States can be bought, has completely permeated our culture. The lead of this article reads, "For the businesses that invested more money than ever before in George W. Bush's costly campaign for the presidency, the returns have already begun." That's quite an accusation, but it's an accusation people don't hesitate to make these days. We should all be saddened by this accusation, perhaps angry at it, but we cannot ignore it or blame the media for it (Feingold 2001).

On the House side, Democratic sponsor Rep. Martin Meehan of Massachusetts argued, "Ending the soft-money system will go a long way towards restoring public confidence in the decisions our government makes. Just as importantly, it will cut the ties between million-dollar contributions and the legislators who write the laws that govern our nation" (Meehan 2002). His Republican counterpart, Rep. Chris Shays of Connecticut, joined the fray by contending, "Our legislation bans soft money, insists that sham 'issue ads' are covered under campaign law, and gives the FEC the teeth necessary to enforce that law" (Shays 2002).

Of course, BCRA had its detractors, chief among them the Republicans' congressional leadership. House Majority Whip Tom DeLay argued:

The McCain-Feingold campaign "reform" bill diminishes individual rights by preventing average citizens from participating in political debates. Americans must understand that if this bill becomes law, it will compromise their freedoms and entrench incumbent politicians. . . . Supporters of McCain-Feingold routinely insinuate that there is widespread political corruption. I reject these claims because the men and women I serve with in Congress are upstanding and honest. Critics make a hollow argument by suggesting that political contributions corrupt elected officials. The central issues in this debate are the preservation of a vibrant freedom of speech and full political participation. I am fighting McCain-Feingold to defend these core constitutional freedoms (DeLay 2001).

Perhaps House Speaker Dennis Hastert of Illinois best punctuated the GOP leadership's opposition to BCRA when he decried it as "Armageddon" for Republicans (Milbank 2002). Although the bill faced stiff opposition primarily because of its soft-money restrictions, some equally important provisions, which raise individual contribution limits, have been largely overlooked. Indeed, one of the pressing questions in campaign finance reform is how political actors will respond to new laws. This question is difficult to answer, prompting calls for caution in the enactment of reforms, lest "unintended consequences" create new problems (Malbin and Gais 1998). Good examples include the proliferation of PACs in the 1970s and 1980s, and the explosion of soft money in the 1980s and 1990s, after the passage of reform bills in 1974 and 1979, respectively. The enactment of BCRA in 2002 offers us a chance to consider the impact of its provisions on the behavior of significant and major donors, which in turn can reveal much about the most aggressive elements of the donor pool.

TABLE 7.6. THE INCREASE IN INDIVIDUAL DONATIONS IF LARGER
CONTRIBUTIONS WERE ALLOWED

	Give More	*Give Same*	*Give Less*
Entire Sample	15%	80	5
Level of Giving:			
Habitual	19%	78	3
Occasional	11%	83	6
Partisanship:			
Republicans	18%	78	5
Independents	14%	80	6
Democrats	11%	85	4
Motives:			
Investors	16%	76	7
Intimates	17%	82	2
Incidentals	14%	78	8
Ideologues	14%	82	3
(N)	(1,025)	(1,025)	(1,025)

Note: Chi-square tests indicate that differences between donors are statistically significant at p<.05 for level of giving and partisanship. Some rows do not add up to 100 percent due to rounding.
Source: The Congressional Donors Survey.

CONTRIBUTOR RESPONSES TO REFORM

In anticipation of the possibility that Congress might some day muster the votes to reform some aspects of the campaign finance system, we asked the donors how they might change their contributions to congressional candidates if larger individual gifts were allowed. Only 15 percent of the significant donors stated they would increase their level of giving, and 80 percent stated that their giving would remain the same (see table 7.6). Five percent reported they would give less: these donors were the most likely to have stated the campaign finance system is broken and were the most critical of elements of the campaign finance system. Habitual donors and wealthier donors were more likely to say that they would give more if the limits were raised, but the most important difference was among partisans.

Fully one-quarter of all strong Republicans said that they would give more if Congress raised the contribution limits, compared with only 12 percent of the strong Democrats (see figure 7.1). Weak Republicans also were likely to maintain that they would give more. If donors who stated they would give more double their giving, and those who say they will give less halve their contributions, then GOP candidates would likely receive 25 percent more contributions from our contributors and Democrats would receive 12 percent more.

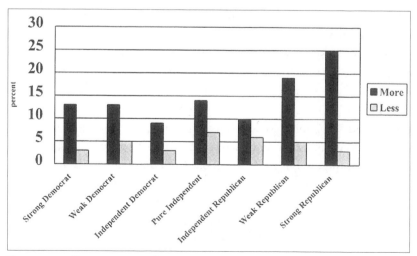

FIGURE 7.1 RESPONSES TO CONTRIBUTION INCREASES BY PARTY
Source: The Congressional Donors Survey.

Of course, candidates, campaign finance directors, and others involved in the fundraising process will change their strategies and their appeals in response to the higher new limits. Democratic solicitors will appeal to Democratic donors to give more to equalize the Republican advantage; some Democratic contributors who say that they will give the same or less may give more in the end. Yet this informed speculation suggests that Republican candidates will be the major beneficiaries of the higher contribution limits.

Summary

One of the ironies of campaign finance reform is that many of the significant donors who fuel the system are very critical of it. There is a strong consensus in favor of replacing or changing the system, substantial agreement on banning soft money and spending limits, but strong disagreement on public subsidies. And ironically the GOP, whose members largely opposed BCRA, is likely to benefit from the provisions of the law that raise individual contribution limits.

Habitual donors, Republicans, and ideologues are more likely to consider campaign contributions to be a legitimate form of participation—one that is motivated by ideology rather than seeking access to officeholders. Occasional donors and Democrats are most likely to perceive political pressure and a quest for access behind donations; ideologues and incidentals also are critical of the system and regard money as especially important in elections.

Donors most critical of the system and Democrats are favorably inclined toward increased regulation and public subsidies of one kind or another. Republicans and habitual donors are more supportive of deregulation. Reforms, such as a ban on soft money, were widely supported among donors and the public. Republicans dominated the small proportion of donors who claim they would increase their donations to candidates, suggesting that the GOP is likely to benefit from these provisions in BCRA.

chapter 8

Conclusion

Money plays a major role in American politics, and individual contributors provide, either directly or indirectly, almost all of the money raised and spent by congressional candidates. However, significant donors who contribute more than $200 to congressional candidates are the least understood participants in the campaign finance system. They have been the focus of this book.

This study has addressed several key questions about the role of individuals who give significant contributions to congressional candidates. First, who contributes? Second, how much do significant donors contribute and to how many candidates? Third, what motivates significant donors to contribute to congressional candidates? Fourth, how do campaigns entice individuals to give? Fifth, who gives to whom? Sixth, are significant donors merely checkbook activists or do they seek to further amplify their voices in politics by contacting members of Congress and their staffs? Finally, how do the donors feel about the campaign finance system in which they participate? The answers to these questions have important implications for American politics.

In chapter 2 we demonstrated that significant contributors are overwhelmingly wealthy, white, middle-aged professionals and businessmen who are integrated into social and political networks. These individuals comprise a relatively stable pool of repeat donors that has relatively few women, young people, and evangelical Christians. There are practically no racial minorities, labor union members, or citizens of modest means in the donor pool. Moreover, the pool has changed little since the 1970s, despite growing demands for money from candidates, the professionalization of the fundraising industry, growing numbers of women and racial minorities holding elected office, and other broad societal changes.

We also showed that most significant donors contribute to only a few candidates, and give modest amounts. Occasional donors comprise half of the donor pool; habitual donors who give to congressional candidates in most elections make up the other half. Most donors give to a House candidate from their own or a neighboring district or to a Senate candidate from their home state. However, a significant number of habitual donors give to many candidates in many localities. Major donors, such as Charles Kushner, who we briefly discussed in a few places, come closest to resembling the stereotypical "fat cat." Major donors are different from significant donors in a few important respects. First, they are more likely to contribute to Democrats than are significant donors–although this Democratic advantage does not offset the Republican edge among habitual and occasional donors. Second, major donors are wealthier and give more money to a greater number of candidates. These donors add an even greater "upper-class accent" to the donor pool.

In the third chapter, we addressed the complicated question of what motivates individuals to make significant contributions to congressional candidates. Some donors are investors who fit the traditional stereotype of self-interested businessmen seeking personal or professional gain. Investors, such as Tom Smith, a retired insurance agent, sometimes become part-time lobbyists for their industry, and often contribute to powerful incumbents across party lines to advance their business interests. Others, however, give for more civic-minded reasons. Many contributors are ideologues; they care deeply about issues that touch people's daily lives, and give to candidates who champion those causes. Recall that Harriet White, for example, cares deeply about environmental protection. Ideologues like her contribute to help elect candidates who will champion their issues and protect their concerns about legislation they deem important, such as a clean water bill. Still others are intimates, such as Dick Jones, who enjoy meeting with friends, colleagues, celebrities, politicians, and other donors at fundraising events. Incidental donors give only occasionally and for idiosyncratic reasons. Those donors, such as Merrill Washington, whom we discussed earlier, may have no interest in politics, but contribute at the behest of a friend or relative, or because of an intense interest in a local problem in their community, or even because of a well-produced direct-mail piece that caught their attention.

Donors tend to take conservative economic stances but disagree on social issues. There are sharp partisan divisions on issues, however, with Democrats taking very liberal positions on most economic and social matters. Republicans take very conservative positions on taxes and spending, but they are divided on social issues such as abortion rights. Partisan donors also are divided in their evaluations of political, economic, and social groups. Republicans are warm toward business associations such as the Chamber of Commerce, but many hold negative views of the Christian Coalition and the NRA. Democrats are favorably disposed toward the Sierra Club and liberal groups. But Democratic donors are relatively cool toward the AFL-CIO, which constitutes a core portion of the party's electoral coalition. This reflects the upper-class business orientation of the donor pool, including Democrats.

Candidates and political consultants are well aware of the biases and motives of significant donors and plan their solicitation strategies accordingly, as we discuss in chapter 4. Campaign finance directors consider the assets and liabilities their candidates bring to a given election, as well as the types of donors who are likely to find those candidates appealing. They select specific solicitation techniques that will bring the candidate the greatest return. One standard practice is to repeatedly target habitual donors with fundraising requests. As a consequence, habitual donors are deluged with solicitations. A second practice is to form finance committees composed of donors who have agreed to raise money from friends, neighbors, and colleagues. As a result, the donor pool reproduces itself; new donors look very much like those who have given in the past. A third practice is to match fundraising appeals to donor motives, resulting in investors being asked to contribute to incumbents who serve on key committees or hold leadership posts, ideologues being inundated with direct-mail and other impersonal solicitations, and intimates receiving numerous personal invitations to fundraising events.

Chapter 5 explored the question of who contributes to whom? Overall, donors are more likely to give to candidates who share their party affiliation and ideology. Incumbency and the competitiveness of the race are also important. However, the most important factor is whether a candidate is running to represent a potential donor, reflecting Tip O'Neill's famous adage, "All politics is local."

Investors contribute more often to incumbents and members who serve on committees they follow closely than do other donors. They care less about whether a candidate shares their ideology or party affiliation. For the typical investor, a contribution is often a means to establish or maintain access to policymakers. Ideologues, by contrast, are much more likely to contribute to candidates who belong to their party and target more of their contributions to candidates in competitive races. They care less than investors and intimates about members' committee assignments. Rather, they consider the election of like-minded politicians their major method for accomplishing their political goals. Intimates are the most likely to contribute to candidates from their state or locality. They also consider the candidates' party and ideology, reflecting their desire to socialize with donors who share their political views.

Typically, the courtship between candidates and donors results in incumbents raising the most contributions from significant donors. Their strong probability of being reelected and ability to influence the policymaking process gives them tremendous advantages in fundraising. Challengers are the inverse of incumbents. Lacking clout in the policy arena and facing long odds of being elected, most challengers raise little money from individual contributors. Some of those who can afford to do so self-finance their campaigns. Open-seat candidates possess few of the advantages of incumbents and few of the disadvantages of challengers. Because of the competitiveness of their races they are usually able to raise substantial sums from significant donors and other sources.

Just as receiving a contribution is important to a candidate, that candidate's ability to get the attention of a member of Congress is important to most donors. In chapter 6, we analyzed the reasons why significant donors contact federal lawmakers and the methods they use. Unlike most citizens, most donors know personally their members of the House and the Senate and have ongoing relationships with them. A majority of the donors personally contact their own members, and a substantial number communicate with other legislators. Most donors get in touch with a member of Congress to express an opinion or acquire information about a bill or policy. Many also contact the people's branch to seek help for themselves, their families or others, or for social reasons. Roughly one out of four acknowledge that they call on legislators for business reasons.

Investors are far more likely than any other group to state that they communicate with members of Congress for business reasons or for help for themselves or family members. They also seek information about specific bills and policies, presumably to determine whether they need to lobby members who serve on the committees they closely follow. Ideologues get in touch with legislators to express their opinions on issues they care about. Intimates contact members for social reasons, but they also seek help for friends and acquaintances. Personal relationships underlie both sets of communications.

In chapter 7, we investigate donors' evaluations about the campaign finance system and their support for reform. Most donors view the system as deeply flawed, and many voice concern about the role of money in elections. Perhaps their most common complaints involve candidates pressuring donors for contributions and donors, in return, pressuring legislators for favors. Despite their ambivalence about the system and the fact that virtually all of them can easily imagine a better campaign finance system, most believe that campaign contributing is a legitimate form of political participation and feel the need to participate in the system that currently exists.

A majority of the donors from both parties favor banning soft money, placing caps on candidate spending, and limiting candidate expenditures on television advertising. A majority of Democrats and a plurality of Republicans also favor banning PAC contributions. Donors are more deeply divided by partisanship over public subsidizing of campaigns and deregulation, but even a majority of Republicans do not favor a laissez-fair approach to campaign finance.

IMPLICATIONS

These findings have important implications for elections, policymaking, and American democracy. Because they contribute significant sums, individual donors have more influence on the conduct of congressional campaigns and the outcomes of elections than do nondonors. The fact that they contribute only to certain candidates means they do little to help other candidates air their arguments during the campaign. Minor-party and independent candidates and long-shot challengers, for example, receive little money from significant donors and therefore have less influence over the political debate.

Overall, significant donors give most of their money to incumbents. Donors' contributions to members of Congress, like those of access-oriented PACs, facilitate incumbents' high reelection rates. Only ideologues are substantially more likely to contribute to candidates, including nonincumbents, in close races.

Significant donors provide a substantial portion of congressional candidates' campaign funds, making them major players in the election process. As a result, candidates spend increasing amounts of time appealing to these donors, interacting with them, and listening to their concerns both during and after the election. Donors clearly have privileged access to members of Congress and their aides. Many follow the policy process closely and do not hesitate to express their views about issues or pending bills. Some work in concert with political parties, interest groups, and informal coalitions. For many investors, particularly those who work in politics, there is a seamless tie between campaigning and governing and between contributing and contacting. For some members of Congress, knowing the interests of their financial constituents is just as important as knowing the opinions of their voting constituents.

Thus significant donors have a greater voice both in elections and the policymaking process than do most other Americans. This is troubling because these individuals constitute a privileged elite. When members of Congress hear more frequently the voice of donors, it creates representational distortion. The degree to which donors hold diverse views on policy and possess different motives for giving serves to mitigate but not eliminate this distortion. The fact that the donor pool is essentially a stable and active political elite means that Congress repeatedly hears the same voices from the same choir. This contributes to the narrow range of policy options that are on the congressional agenda.

CAMPAIGN FINANCE REFORM

The Bipartisan Campaign Finance Reform Act of 2002 will increase the amount of money significant donors can give directly to congressional candidates. The wealthiest donors are the most likely to take advantage of the opportunity to contribute more, potentially increasing the representational distortion in the political system. Moreover, because Republican donors are more likely to say that they will give more if the limits are raised, voices advocating conservative economic policies will become louder and those advocating social welfare policies will become less audible.

What can be done to mitigate representational distortion? One possibility is to reduce the demand for contributions and increase the supply of campaign funds. The public financing of congressional elections would certainly reduce the influence of significant donors and interest groups in elections and policy making, but it is unlikely that a public funding program will be enacted in the near future. Other things can be done short of a massive restructuring of the campaign finance system. Some possibilities include providing candidates with free or subsidized television or radio time or postage. This would reduce the impact of money, including individual contributions, on elections. It also would lessen the amount of time candidates spend raising money, including meeting with significant donors.

In addition, the tax code could be used to stimulate contributions from a wider variety of donors. Citizens of modest means might be more willing to contribute to congressional candidates if they received tax credits for every dollar they contribute up to $200 and lesser credits for additional contributions. The creation of a larger pool of potential donors might encourage professional fundraisers to invest more effort prospecting for contributions among less affluent voters, thereby increasing the size and diversity of the donor pool.

Regardless of the impact of BCRA and the potential for enacting additional reforms, this book has demonstrated that individuals play important roles in financing congressional elections. Significant donors, like political parties and interest groups, bring a variety of goals and motives to the political arena. Candidates and fundraising professionals cater to donor preferences when raising money and maintain ongoing relationships with them once an election is over. Indeed, the courtship between candidates and significant congressional donors is a critical part of American politics.

Methodology

Our goal in writing this book was to make a systematic and comprehensive assessment of individuals who contribute at least $200 to one congressional candidate and of the processes that lead them to make contributions. We sought to address several overarching questions: Who are these individuals? How much do significant donors contribute and to how many candidates? What motivates significant donors to contribute to congressional candidates? How do campaigns entice individuals to give? Who gives to whom? Are significant donors merely checkbook activists or do they seek to further amplify their voice in politics by contacting members of Congress and their staffs? Finally, how do the donors feel about the campaign finance system in which they participate?

DATA SOURCES

Our primary statistical analysis is based upon a survey of individuals who contributed $200 to one or more candidates competing in the 1996 congressional elections. The names, addresses, and contribution information for these individuals were obtained from the Federal Election Commission. The first wave of the survey was mailed in August 1997. Two follow-ups were sent to individuals who did not respond to the earlier mailings. The response rate was 47 percent, excluding undeliverable questionnaires.

Several data sets were constructed from these data. The first uses each individual survey response as the unit of analysis. Responses are weighted in inverse proportion to the number of times each contributor appeared on the FEC lists to correct for the over-representation of frequent givers that would otherwise result from a simple sample of contributions. In addition, the data were weighed to correct for differences in response rates among various types of contributors.

A logistic regression was used to predict whether or not a contributor responded to the survey, using region, the size of the contribution, the amount of the
contribution, the party of the candidate to whom the contribution was made,
and the contributor's gender. Cases were weighted to correct for the under-rep-
resentation of types of contributors as indicated by the logistic coefficients.

A second data set, used for the analysis in table 4.4, was constructed by pairing survey respondents with candidates from whom the donors recalled receiving a fundraising solicitation. This included a maximum of three candidates
whom donors reported that they received a solicitation from and made a contribution to, and a maximum of three candidates whom they reported receiving a
solicitation from but did not make a contribution to (leaving a possible total of
six different candidates paired with each donor). The unit of analysis is each possible donor-candidate/solicitation combination, which provides us with a matrix
of 2,104 cases (or 2,967 weighted cases) with full information for each variable
specified in the models.

A third data set was constructed by combining the donor survey data with
the FEC records for the contributions these individuals made to 1996 House and
Senate candidates and information about the candidate's background, including
incumbents' committee assignments and nonincumbents' previous political experience. For all candidates, we gathered information about party affiliation, ideology (provided by Ansolabehere, Snyder, and Stewart 2001), and electoral competitiveness. There were 642 survey respondents who returned their
questionnaires with identification numbers attached, who had given to one or
more general-election candidates rather than to only primary candidates, and
who could be located in the Federal Election Commission records. These
donors were then paired with each of the 1,003 major-party House and Senate
candidates who competed in the 1996 general election and Senate incumbents
who were not up for reelection. At this point, we calculated several candidate-
donor variables, including party agreement, ideological similarity, and an indication as to whether or not the congressional committee on which an incumbent
served matched a committee the donor followed.

The data set has 869 major-party House candidates who competed in the
1996 general election. A Texas court order mandated redistricting in August
1996. This resulted in six districts (TX-8, TX-9, TX-19, TX-24, TX-25, and
TX-30) which held general election contests with multiple major-party candidacies. Because these candidates all competed in the November election, we included them in our analysis. In addition, given the unique runoff process in
Louisiana elections, we treated their October election as the general election,
but we included in our analysis only the top two finishers from each primary.
Our analysis also includes sixty-eight Senate candidates who ran for reelection
and sixty-six Senate incumbents who were not up for reelection in 1996.

For each donor, we created a case for every House and Senate candidate in
the United States. The unit of analysis is each possible donor-candidate combi-

nation, which provides us with a matrix of 643,926 cases (or 656,416 weighted cases). Some cases were dropped because of missing values on some variables. Of these candidate-donor pairings, it should be noted that only 1,260 consisted of actual campaign contributions. These data were used to model the contribution decision in chapter 5, where the dependent variable indicates whether or not a respondent gave to that particular candidate or not.

A similar technique was used to construct a fourth data set that was used to assess which donors sought to influence the policy process by contacting members of Congress (or their aides). For each donor we created a case for every member of the House and Senate. The unit of analysis is each possible donor-member combination, which provides us with a matrix of 408,158 cases (or 415,071 weighted cases). These data were used to model the decision to contact a member of Congress in chapter 6, where the dependent variables indicate whether or not donors contacted their own members or other members for different reasons.

In addition, we make limited use, primarily in terms of comparison, of other survey data collected from congressional donors. These data sets were primarily collected by various combinations of the authors of the current survey. Each survey is identified when it is discussed in the analysis. Our most frequent reference is to a small survey of major donors—those who made eight or more contributions to congressional candidates and/or contributed a total of $8,000 or more to congressional candidates. This sample consists of a survey of individuals identified as major donors from the amounts of their 1990 contributions (Wilcox et al. 1998) who remained major donors in 1996 combined with those respondents in our survey of 1996 donors who made sufficient contributions to be defined as major donors. In both cases, the determination of their status as major donors in 1996 was made by their answers to a survey of items asking how many House and Senate candidates they gave to in 1996 and the sizes of these contributions.

Other data we use for comparisons consist of a survey we replicated for a sample of individuals who contributed to House candidates during the 1978 election. This survey allowed us to make some limited over-time panel comparisons from 1978 to 1996. (The details of the 1978 survey were described in Powell 1982 and 1989). More than 40 percent of the 1978 sample were 55 and over in 1979 when they were first surveyed, and many of the individuals in this sample were ill or deceased when we attempted to resurvey them 18 years later in 1997. And, of course, after 18 years, some individuals could not be located. We had possible addresses from purchased phone directories for 64 percent of the original 1,212 nonanonymous respondents. Of the original 1,212 nonanonymous respondents, 266 were successfully resurveyed. The respondents' gender and year of birth were matched in both surveys to ensure we had the same individual—54 surveys were discarded because of mismatches, leaving the 212 remaining correct matches. We also checked the FEC contribution records for all 1,212 original respondents from 1978 through 1994, allowing us to examine the duration, frequency, amount, partisanship and recipients (House candidates, Senate candidates, Presidential candidates, parties, and PACs) of their donations.

To add context and depth to our discussion, we conducted semi-structured interviews with 32 significant congressional donors. Of the donors we interviewed, 31 responded to our survey and one was a lobbyist in Washington, D.C. Most of the interviews were conducted by telephone, although some were completed in person. The interviews occurred in May and June of 1998 and lasted from fifteen to sixty minutes. The typical interview took twenty minutes. Respondents were asked open-ended questions concerning their general involvement in politics, the reasons they contribute money to political candidates, how often they contribute money to candidates, how many candidates solicit them, the types of solicitations they receive and respond to, and their assessments of the campaign finance system and reform.

Finally, we collected information about the fundraising process from experts in the field. We conducted interviews with six of the nation's leading professional campaign finance directors, three of whom work for Democrats and three of whom work for Republicans. We collected a large number of fundraising materials, including letters and invitations to events. Several of us also helped to organize fundraising events and one of us drew from his experience organizing a fundraising event for an incumbent House member.

Items in the Congressional Mail Survey

Our survey contained a variety of attitudinal, behavioral, and demographic items (see figure A-1). We asked the respondents for their views on a variety of political issues, using five-point strong-agree / strong-disagree formats. Respondents were also asked about their partisanship and liberalism-conservatism on seven-point scales. Feeling thermometer scores on a 0-to-100 scale were also obtained for a variety of groups and individuals—conservatives, liberals, Republican party, Democratic party, Christian Coalition, Chamber of Commerce, NOW, AFL-CIO, NRA, Sierra Club, Newt Gingrich, and Bill Clinton. We focused on specific attitudes relevant to the contribution decision. Finally, we asked about attitudes towards a variety of campaign reform measures. (The details of these items are provided in chapter 7.)

Figure A. Congressional Campaign Finance Study

Please answer as many of the following questions as possible by marking the appropriate space or filling in the blank provided. Please return the questionnaire in the enclosed envelope. Thank you for your time and assistance.

1. What are your views on the following political issues?

	Strongly Agree	Agree	Neutral	Disagree	Strongly Disagree
a. Taxes should be cut even if it means reducing public services.	(1)	(2)	(3)	(4)	(5)
b. Homosexuals should be allowed to teach in the public schools.	(1)	(2)	(3)	(4)	(5)
c. The U.S. needs a comprehensive national health insurance program.	(1)	(2)	(3)	(4)	(5)
d. Abortion should be outlawed except to save the mother's life.	(1)	(2)	(3)	(4)	(5)
e. The federal government should spend more to reduce poverty and hunger in the U.S.	(1)	(2)	(3)	(4)	(5)
f. More environmental protection is needed even if it raises prices or costs jobs.	(1)	(2)	(3)	(4)	(5)
g. The country has gone too far in helping African Americans and other minorities.	(1)	(2)	(3)	(4)	(5)
h. The U.S. should sharply reduce defense spending.	(1)	(2)	(3)	(4)	(5)
i. Free trade is important even if it means the loss of U.S. jobs.	(1)	(2)	(3)	(4)	(5)
j. The U.S. should return to the gold standard.	(1)	(2)	(3)	(4)	(5)
k. Women should have an equal role with men in business, industry, and government.	(1)	(2)	(3)	(4)	(5)

2. Generally speaking, do you consider yourself to be a:

Strong						Strong
Republican			Independent			Democrat
(1)	(2)	(3)	(4)	(5)	(6)	(7)

3. How would you describe your political views? What about the views of your U.S. Senators and U.S. House member? If you do not know their views well, please check "Don't Know." **Please fill in the names of your U.S. Senators and U.S. House member.**

	Don't Know	Extremely Liberal	Liberal	Slightly Liberal	Moderate/ Middle of the Road	Slightly Conser- vative	Conser- vative	Extremely Conser- vative
YOUR-SELF	( )	(1)	(2)	(3)	(4)	(5)	(6)	(7)
_____ **Senator**	( )	(1)	(2)	(3)	(4)	(5)	(6)	(7)
_____ **Senator**	( )	(1)	(2)	(3)	(4)	(5)	(6)	(7)
_____ **House**	( )	(1)	(2)	(3)	(4)	(5)	(6)	(7)

4. How frequently have you **contributed money** to candidates, parties or PACs, **AND** how frequently have you **worked** for any of them (for example by organizing fundraisers or rallies)?

	CONTRIBUTED TO:			WORKED FOR:		
	Most Elections	Some Elections	Never	Most Elections	Some Elections	Never
a. Presidential candidates	(1)	(2)	(3)	(1)	(2)	(3)
b. U.S. Senate candidates	(1)	(2)	(3)	(1)	(2)	(3)
c. U.S. House candidates	(1)	(2)	(3)	(1)	(2)	(3)
d. State/local candidates	(1)	(2)	(3)	(1)	(2)	(3)
e. Political parties	(1)	(2)	(3)	(1)	(2)	(3)
f. PACs	(1)	(2)	(3)	(1)	(2)	(3)

5. Have you ever asked other people to make a contribution to any of the following?

Presidential candidate	(1) Yes	(2) No	Congressional candidate	(1) Yes	(2) No
Party committee	(1) Yes	(2) No	PAC	(1) Yes	(2) No

6. In 1996, approximately how many candidates for the U.S. Senate or U.S. House of Representatives **ASKED** you for a campaign contribution?

( ) None   ( ) One   ( ) Two to five   ( ) Six to ten   ( ) More than ten

7. In 1996, approximately how many candidates for U.S. Senate or U.S. House of Representative **DID YOU** contribute to?

( ) None   ( ) One   ( ) Two to five   ( ) Six to ten   ( ) More than ten

8. In 1996, approximately **HOW MANY** U.S. House or U.S. Senate candidates did you contribute to in the following dollar ranges?

_____ $200 or less   _____ $201 to $500   _____ $501 to $999   _____$1000

9. If you **DID CONTRIBUTE** to any U.S. House or U.S. Senate candidates in 1996, **please list the names and states of candidates you contributed to** (list no more than three). Please answer the following questions by marking all spaces that apply for each candidate listed.

WAS THE REQUEST:	from someone you knew personally? Yes	an invitation to an event? Yes	in person? Yes	by mail? Yes	by phone? Yes
a._____ name (state)	( )	( )	( )	( )	( )
b._____ name (state)	( )	( )	( )	( )	( )
c._____ name (state)	( )	( )	( )	( )	( )

10. Please list names and states of U.S. House or U.S. Senate candidates **WHO ASKED YOU** for a contribution in 1996, but to whom you **DID NOT** contribute (list no more than three). Please answer the following questions by marking all spaces that apply for each candidate listed.

WAS THE REQUEST:	from someone you knew personally? Yes	an invitation to an event? Yes	in person? Yes	by mail? Yes	by phone? Yes
a._____ name (state)	( )	( )	( )	( )	( )
b._____ name (state)	( )	( )	( )	( )	( )
c._____ name (state)	( )	( )	( )	( )	( )

11. If you are **asked** to make a contribution by people you **KNOW PERSONALLY,** how well do the following statements describe the occasions on which you **make** contributions?

		I CONTRIBUTE		
WHEN ASKED BY:	Often	Occasionally	Seldom	Never
a. Friend or relative	(1)	(2)	(3)	(4)
b. A candidate	(1)	(2)	(3)	(4)
c. A member of a candidate's staff	(1)	(2)	(3)	(4)
d. Co-worker or member of my profession	(1)	(2)	(3)	(4)
e Someone I do business with	(1)	(2)	(3)	(4)
f. Someone in my place of worship	(1)	(2)	(3)	(4)

g. Someone in a social group I belong to	(1)	(2)	(3)	(4)
h. Someone in a political group I belong to	(1)	(2)	(3)	(4)
i. Someone in my political party	(1)	(2)	(3)	(4)

12. How important are the following factors in your decision to make a contribution to a U.S. House or U.S. Senate candidate?

	Always Important	Sometimes Important	Seldom Important
a. Candidate is from my district or state	(1)	(2)	(3)
b. I know the candidate personally	(1)	(2)	(3)
c. Candidate's liberalism-conservatism	(1)	(2)	(3)
d. So my business will be treated fairly	(1)	(2)	(3)
e. Candidate is in a close race	(1)	(2)	(3)
f. Asked by someone I know personally	(1)	(2)	(3)
g. Candidate's party	(1)	(2)	(3)
h. Candidate is friendly to my industry or work	(1)	(2)	(3)
i. Candidate is likely to win the election	(1)	(2)	(3)
j. Asked by someone I don't want to say no to	(1)	(2)	(3)
k. Candidate's position on a specific issue	(1)	(2)	(3)
l. Involves an event I want to attend	(1)	(2)	(3)
m. Candidate's opponent is unacceptable	(1)	(2)	(3)
n. People in my line of work are giving	(1)	(2)	(3)
o. A group I respect supports the candidate	(1)	(2)	(3)
p. Candidate's seniority, committee or leadership position	(1)	(2)	(3)

13. How important to you are the following reasons for making a campaign contribution to U.S. House and U.S. Senate candidates?

	Very Important	Somewhat Important	Not Very Important
a. To influence the policies of government	(1)	(2)	(3)
b. It is expected of someone in my position	(1)	(2)	(3)
c. For business or employment reasons	(1)	(2)	(3)
d. Enjoyment of the friendship and social contacts	(1)	(2)	(3)
e. To make a difference in the outcome of an election	(1)	(2)	(3)
f. It gives me a feeling of recognition	(1)	(2)	(3)
g. To support a candidate or cause	(1)	(2)	(3)

14. Please rate the following individuals, groups, or organizations on a scale from **0 to 100**, where **0** is **most unfavorable**, **100** is **most favorable**, and **50** is **neutral**, and you may use the entire 0 to 100 scale. If you have no opinion or knowledge of the person or group, please place an **X** on the line.

a. Bill Clinton _____   e. Liberals _____   i. Republican Party _____

b. Newt Gingrich _____   f. Conservatives _____   j. Democratic Party _____

c. Sierra Club _____   g. NOW _____   k. Christian Coalition _____

d. NRA _____   h. AFL-CIO _____   l. Chamber of Commerce _____

15. Are you a member of any of the following kinds of organizations? (Check all that apply.)

( ) business   ( ) gun owner   ( ) women's

( ) environmental   ( ) party   ( ) fraternal

( ) pro-family   ( ) conservative   ( ) community

( ) civic   ( ) pro-life   ( ) liberal

( ) pro-choice   ( ) professional   ( ) labor union

( ) church   ( ) civil rights   ( ) Christian conservative

16. Have you ever made out a check to a candidate but let an organization deliver it for you?

(1) No   (2) Yes

IF YES, the organization was: _____

name

17. Are any of the following sources of information important to you in deciding which U.S. House or U.S. Senate candidates to contribute to? (Check all that are important.)

( ) political newsletters   ( ) newspapers

( ) labor unions   ( ) business, industry, trade groups

( ) candidates, campaigns   ( ) party organizations

( ) religious groups   ( ) issue, ideological groups

18. Are there any **GROUPS** that are especially helpful to you in deciding on candidates to contribute to? Please list specific names.

1. _____   2. _____   3. _____

name   name   name

19. During the last two years, how many members of the U.S. House of Representatives, U.S. Senate, or their staffs have you **CONTACTED?**

HOUSE   ( ) None   ( ) One   ( ) Two to Five   ( ) Six to ten   ( ) More than ten

SENATE   ( ) None   ( ) One   ( ) Two to Five   ( ) Six to ten   ( ) More than ten

20. Have you contacted the U.S. House member from your district?

(1) No   (2) Yes

21. Have you contacted the U.S. Senators from your state?

( ) None   ( ) One   ( ) Both

22. I AM PERSONALLY ACQUAINTED WITH:

My U.S. House member	(1) Yes	(2) No
One of my U.S. Senators	(1) Yes	(2) No
Both of my U.S. Senators	(1) Yes	(2) No

23. Please list the names and states of U.S. House members or U.S. Senators you have contacted in the last two years (list no more than three). What was the nature of the contacts? Please mark all statements that apply for each official listed.

	1. _____		2. _____		3. _____	
	name	(state)	name	(state)	name	(state)
a. To express an opinion on a bill	**Yes** ( )		**Yes** ( )		**Yes** ( )	
b. To express an opinion on a policy	( )		( )		( )	
c. To seek information on a bill or a policy	( )		( )		( )	
d. To seek help for you or your family on a problem	( )		( )		( )	
e. To seek help for someone else on a problem	( )		( )		( )	
f. For social reasons	( )		( )		( )	
g. Did any of the above contacts relate to your job or business?	( )		( )		( )	

24. Have you ever done anything to try to influence an Act of Congress? (Check all that apply)

(1) No **YES, I HAVE:**
( ) Written to Senators or House members
( ) Spoken with Senators or House members
( ) Spoken with the staff of Senators or House members
( ) Worked through a political party
( ) Worked through formal groups other than parties
( ) Worked through informal groups
( ) Testified before Congress

25. What issues particularly interest you?

1. _____
2. _____
3. _____

26. Do you follow closely the activities of any particular House or Senate committees?

(1) No (2) Yes

IF YES, which committees?

House: _____

Senate: _____

BACKGROUND INFORMATION

27. State of residence _____   28. Year of birth _____

29. Gender: (1) Male   (2) Female

30. Race/ethnicity: (1) White   (2) African American   (3) Hispanic   (4) Asian   (5) Other

31. Religious denomination: (Please be specific)

_____

32. How often do you attend religious services?

(1)	(2)	(3)	(4)	(5)
More than once a week	Once a week	Several times a month	A few times a year	Seldom/ Never

33. Education:

(1)	(2)	(3)	(4)	(5)
High School Or less degree	Some College	College Graduate	Some Graduate	Graduate Degree _____

34. Family income:

(1)	(2)	(3)	(4)	(5)
Less than $50,000	$50,000– $99,999	$100,000– $249,999	$250,000– $500,000	Above $500,000

35. Current occupation (or former if retired):

_____   (1) Current   (2) Retired

36. In what **business or industry** do you or did you work?

_____

37. As part of your job, are you involved in politics or government?   (1) No   (2) Yes

IF YES, are you:

(1)	(2)	(3)	(4)	(5)	(6)
Elected/appointed Officeholder	Lobbyist/ Public Relations	Party Official	Political Consultant	PAC Official	Gov't Staffer/ Civil Servant

CAMPAIGN FINANCE REFORM

38. When you think about how campaigns are paid for, which statement **BEST** reflects your view of the current campaign finance system?

    (1) It is broken and needs to be replaced.

    (2) It has problems and needs to be changed.

    (3) It has some problems but is basically sound.

    (4) It is all right just the way it is and should not be changed.

39. Please indicate your views on each of these statements on the role of money in politics.

	Strongly Agree	Agree	Neutral	Disagree	Strongly Disagree
a. Office holders regularly pressure donors for money	(1)	(2)	(3)	(4)	(5)
b. Donors regularly pressure elected officials for favors	(1)	(2)	(3)	(4)	(5)
c. Contributing is a legitimate form of participation	(1)	(2)	(3)	(4)	(5)
d. Most donors are seeking access to government	(1)	(2)	(3)	(4)	(5)
e. Most donors are motivated by ideology	(1)	(2)	(3)	(4)	(5)
f. Money is the single most important factor in elections	(1)	(2)	(3)	(4)	(5)

40. What are your views on the following campaign finance reforms?

	Strongly Agree	Agree	Neutral	Disagree	Strongly Disagree
a. Placing a limit on spending-by congressional candidates	(1)	(2)	(3)	(4)	(5)
b. Limit TV advertising of congressional candidates	(1)	(2)	(3)	(4)	(5)
c. Provide public funding for congressional candidates	(1)	(2)	(3)	(4)	(5)
d. Eliminate large "soft money" contributions	(1)	(2)	(3)	(4)	(5)
e. Ban PACs from giving money to congressional candidates	(1)	(2)	(3)	(4)	(5)
f. Allow individuals to make larger gifts to candidates	(1)	(2)	(3)	(4)	(5)
g. Eliminate all limitations and require full disclosure	(1)	(2)	(3)	(4)	(5)
h. Allow parties to make larger gifts to candidates	(1)	(2)	(3)	(4)	(5)
i. Give free media time and postage to candidates	(1)	(2)	(3)	(4)	(5)

41. How might your own contributions to congressional candidates be affected if the following changes were enacted?

	Would you give:		
	More	Same	Less
If PAC contributions were not allowed?	(1)	(2)	(3)
If larger individual gifts were allowed?	(1)	(2)	(3)

Thank you for your time and consideration!

We asked respondents detailed questions about their political contributing behavior. We asked them how often they contributed, to whom they contributed, and how often they worked for: presidential, Senate, and House candidates; state and local candidates; political parties; and PACs. We also asked how many 1996 House and Senate candidates solicited them and to how many they contributed, along with the amounts they contributed. The respondents also were asked who specifically solicited them for a contribution (including up to three candidates to whom they contributed and up to three candidates to whom they refused to contribute) and how they were asked (by someone they knew personally; in person, by mail or by phone; and whether or not the request involved an invitation to an event). They also were asked if they had ever asked other individuals to make a contribution to: presidential candidates; party committees; congressional candidates; or PACs.

We asked the respondents to indicate how often they contributed when asked by someone they knew personally who was a friend or relative; candidate; member of candidate's staff; coworker or member of their profession; someone they do business with; someone in their place of worship; someone in a social group to which they belong; someone in a political group to which they belong; someone in their political party. They were asked how important each of the following factors was in their decision to make a contribution to a U.S. House or U.S. Senate candidate: candidate is from their district or state; they know the candidate personally; candidate's liberalism-conservatism; so their business will be treated fairly; candidate is in a close race; asked by someone they know personally; candidate's party; candidate is friendly to their industry or work; candidate is likely to win the election; asked by someone they don't want to say no to; candidate's position on a specific issue; involves an event they want to attend; candidate's opponent is unacceptable; people in their line of work are giving; a group they respect supports the candidate; the candidate's seniority, committee, or leadership position. They also were asked how important the following reasons were for making a campaign contribution: to influence the policies of government; it is expected of someone in their position; for business or employment reasons; enjoyment of the friendship and social contacts; to make a difference in the outcome of an election; it gives them a feeling of recognition; to support a candidate or cause.

The respondents also were asked whether they ever made out a check to a candidate but let an organization deliver it for them. They were asked about the sources of information that were important to them in deciding to which candidates to contribute: political newsletters; labor unions; candidates, campaigns; religious groups; newspapers; business or industry, trade groups; party organizations; issues or ideological groups. Furthermore, they were asked if there were any specific groups that were helpful in deciding which candidates to contribute to. They also were asked about their membership in a variety of organizations.

The respondents were asked how many House members, Senate members, or congressional aides they contacted in the last two years. They were asked specifically if they had contacted the House member from their district or the senator from their state. Then, they were asked to list up to three specific members they had contacted. For each member with whom they communicated, they were asked whether their contact was: to express an opinion on a bill; to express an opinion on a policy; to seek information on a bill or a policy; to seek help for themselves or their family on a problem; to seek help for someone else on a problem; for social reasons.

They were asked if any of the preceding contacts related to their job or business. They were also asked if they have ever done anything to influence an act of Congress: written to Senators or House members; spoken with senators or House members; spoken with the staff of senators or House members; worked through a political party; worked through formal groups other than a party; worked through informal groups; testified before Congress. The respondents were asked if they were personally acquainted with their House members or senators. They also were queried as to whether or not they closely follow the activities of any particular House or Senate committees, and if yes, which committees. We also asked the respondents about their age, gender, race, religion, education, family income, and occupation.

The motives and typology of the contributors are based on a factor analysis of items asking about the importance of a variety of possible reasons for making contributions to House or Senate candidates. The possible reasons are: candidate's liberalism-conservatism; so one's business will be treated fairly; candidate is friendly to one's business or work; involves an event one wants to attend; people in one's line of work are giving; to influence the policies of government; it is expected of someone in the contributor's position; for business or employment reasons; enjoyment of friendship and social contacts; to make a difference in the election outcome; feeling of recognition; to support a candidate or cause. Three rotated (oblimin) factors were extracted defining the purposive, material, and solidary factors. Donors were categorized as ideologues, investors, or intimates based on their highest factor score. If all their factor scores were below average, then they were placed in a fourth category for the relatively unmotivated, referred to as incidentals.

Data Analysis Techniques

Several statistical techniques were used to analyze the data collected for this book. The first and most basic set of results came from cross-tabulations, which relied on Chi-Square tests to determine statistical significance. Second, bivariate correlations were used to generate the results for the figures in chapter 3. Kendall's Tau-b correlations were used for ordinal variables and Pearson correlations were used for continuous or dummy variables.

We used six multivariate techniques in various chapters of the book. Factor analysis was used to identify the underlying dimensions of several sets of variables and to create factor scores that were used in ensuing analysis (see

Kline 2000). Cluster analysis was used to group donors according to their views on different political organizations (see Lorr 1987). We used ordinary least-squares regression for causal analyses involving an interval-dependent variable. We used ordered probit analysis when the dependent variable was ordinal (see Long and Freese 2001) and logistic regression analysis when the dependent variable was binary and normally distributed (see Agresti 1990). We employed rare-events logit when the dependent variable was binary and there was a far greater number of zeros (or nonevents) than ones (or events). Logistic regression or probit analysis can underestimate the probability of the event under this condition. Rare-events logit corrects for the problem and has been shown to outperform other techniques (see King and Zeng 2001). We calculated conditional effects to make the results more readily interpretable when using nonlinear estimation techniques.

TABLE A-1. THE ESTIMATED PROBABILITY THAT SIGNIFICANT DONORS RECEIVE SIX OR MORE SOLICITATIONS

Material motives	—
Purposive motives	+ 7%
Solidary motives	—
Habitual donor	+ 13%
Membership in number of types of groups	+ 6%
Asked others to give	—
Political job	+ 12%
Number of members contacted	+ 36%
Woman	+ 8%
Evangelical	—
Catholic	—
Jewish	+ 17%
Strong partisan	+ 6%
Democratic partisanship	—
Education	+ 11%
Income	+ 28%
Refused income	+ 16%
Age	—

Note: The designation "—" indicates that the variable is not a statistically significant predictor for the number of solicitations received by significant donors. Estimates are based on the ordered probit analysis in table 4.1.
Source: The Congressional Donors Survey.

TABLE A-2. THE ESTIMATED PROBABILITY OF CONTACTING SIX OR MORE MEMBERS OF CONGRESS

	House	Senate
Material motives	—	—
Purposive motives	—	+ 2%
Solidary motives	—	—
Habitual donor	+ 7%	+ 5%
Membership in number of types of groups	+ 8%	+ 7%
Asked others to give	+ 7%	+ 2%
Political job	—	—
Strong partisan	—	—
Democratic partisanship	—	—
Donor follows congressional committee	+ 11%	+ 6%
Education	—	—
Income	+ 5%	+ 6%
Refused income	—	—
N		

Note: The designation "—" indicates that the variable is not a statistically significant predictor for contacting six or more members of Congress during the last two years. Estimates are based on the ordered probit analysis in table 6.1.
Source: The Congressional Donors Survey.

Table A-3. The Estimated Probability of Contacting One's Own Member of Congress

	Opinion bill	Opinion policy	Info bill/ policy	Business reasons	Help you or family	Help someone else	Social reasons
Material motives	—	—	+ 6%	+ 28%	+ 2%	—	—
Purposive motives	+ 18%	+ 16%	—	—	—	—	+ 3%
Solidary motives	– 7%	– 7%	—	—	—	+ 4%	+ 5%
Party agreement	+ 9%	+ 12%	+ 8%	+ 8%	—	+ 6%	+ 5%
Political independent	—	—	—	+ 7%	—	—	+ 9%
Ideological similarity	+ 14%	+ 17%	—	—	+ 6%	—	—
Senate candidate	+ 8%	—	—	—	—	—	—
Senate candidate not up for reelection	– 14%	– 12%	– 7%	– 8%	—	– 3%	– 4%
Donor follows congressional committee	—	+ 9%	+ 6%	—	—	—	—
Committee match	—	—	—	—	—	—	—
Habitual donor	—	+ 5%	—	—	—	—	—
Income	—	—	—	+ 11%	—	+ 4%	+ 8%
Refused income	—	– 18%	—	—	—	—	—

Note: The designation "__" indicates that the variable is not a statistically significant predictor of contacting one's own member of Congress. Estimates are based on the logistic regression analysis in table 6.2.
Source: The Congressional Donors Survey.

TABLE A-4. THE ESTIMATED LIKELIHOOD OF CONTACTING A MEMBER OF CONGRESS OUTSIDE DISTRICT

	Opinion bill	Opinion policy	Info bill/ policy	Business reasons	Help someone else	Social reasons
Material motives	—	—	+3.0 times	+4.0 times	+2.3 times	—
Purposive motives	—	—	-1.7 times	+1.6 times	—	—
Solidary motives	—	—	—	—	—	+1.6 times
Party agreement	+2.0 times	+2 times	—	—	+4.0 times	+3.6 times
Political independent	+1.6 times	+1.9 times	—	+1.8 times	—	—
Ideological similarity	+3.3 times	+5.8 times	—	+6.3 times	+24 times	—
Senate candidate	—	—	—	—	+3.8 times	+4.0 times
Senate candidate not up for reelection	—	—	—	—	—	—
Donor follows congressional committee	+1.7 times	+2.5 times	+4.2 times	+2.7 times	—	+2.0 times
Committee match	+2.9 times	+3.2 times	—	+3.1 times	+3.9 times	+5.0 times
Habitual donor	—	—	—	—	—	-2.2 times
Income	—	—	—	—	—	+4.5 times
Refused income	—	+1.8 times	—	—	+5.3 times	—

Note: The designation "—" indicates that the variable is not a statistically significant predictor of contacting one's own member of Congress. Estimates are based on rare-events logit analysis in table 6.3.
Source: The Congressional Donors Survey.

TABLE A-5. THE ESTIMATED PROBABILITY OF INFLUENCING AN ACT OF CONGRESS

	Written to member of Congress	Spoken with member	Spoken with staff	Worked through Party	Worked formal group	Worked informal group	Testified before Congress
Material motives	—	+ 14%	.+ 11%	—	+ 13%	—	+ 4%
Purposive motives	+ 16%	+ 8%	+ 17%	+ 16%	+ 17%	+ 10%	—
Solidary motives	—	—	—	+ 14%	—	+ 3%	+ 5%
Habitual donor	—	+ 16%	+ 18%	—	—	—	—
Membership in number of types of groups	+ 23%	+ 30%	+ 21%	+ 22%	+ 25%	—	+ 7%
Asked others to give	+ 9%	+ 21%	+ 18%	+ 12%	—	+ 8%	—
Political job	—	—	—	—	—	—	—
Strong partisan	—	—	—	+ 18%	+ 12%	—	—
Democratic partisanship	—	—	—	—	+ 25%	+ 11%	—
Donor follows congressional committee	+ 12%	+ 26%	+ 20%	+ 8%	+ 21%	+ 15%	+ 15%
Education	+ 20%	—	—	—	+ 19%	—	+ 6%
Income	—	—	—	—	+ 25%	+ 11%	—
Refused income	—	—	—	—	—	—	—
Age	+ 7%	—	—	—	—	—	+ 11%

Note: The designation "__" indicates that the variable is not a statistically significant predictor for influencing an act of Congress. Estimates are based on the logistic regression analysis in table 6.4.
Source: The Congressional Donors Survey.

Notes

1. Introduction

1. This estimate was provided by the staff of the Center for Responsive Politics in a personal communication, based on their analysis of donors.

2. In an effort to exclude the impact of minor-party candidates, all figures in this chapter refer to major-party candidates in two-party contested general elections unless otherwise noted.

3. With the exceptions of Steve Forbes in 1996 and 2000, and Texas governors John Connelly in 1980 and George W. Bush in 2000, every aspirant for a major party nomination has participated in the federal matching funds program since it was first instituted as part of the FECA. Every major-party presidential nominee has accepted federal funding during the general election.

4. This paraphrases Schattschneider's (1960) observation about the bias of pluralism.

2. Who Are the Financiers of Congressional Elections?

1. The 1978 survey sampled House contributors who gave $101 or more to a congressional candidate. They were counted as contributors in the 1990s if they gave $200 or more in 1990 or 1992 or $250 in 1994. These differences are a function of changing FEC disclosure requirements.

2. Respondents were asked: "How frequently have you contributed money to candidates . . . U.S. Senate, U.S. House . . . in most elections, some elections, never?"

3. The 1978 survey randomly selected 24 contributors per candidate in the roughly 100 districts studied in the 1978 National Election Study. These re-

spondents were drawn from lists of contributors provided by the Federal Election Commission.

4. Both "women's groups" and "pro-family groups" have slightly ambiguous meanings. There are conservative women's groups such as Concerned Women for America, and liberal pro-family groups such as the Children's Defense Fund.

3. What Motivates Donors?

1. In addition, there were too few donors in the survey for us to analyze them as independent subgroups.

2. This is a very conservative position, albeit more liberal than the GOP Republican platform.

3. Since the social desirability of gender equality is so strongly established, it is likely that a neutral response represents opposition to equality.

4. Donors were classified into different partisan constituencies based on cluster analysis. The cluster analysis was based on donors' responses to questions on economic and cultural issues, donors' feeling-thermometer ratings of various interest groups, and donors' involvement in various political groups.

4. Candidates, Donors, and Fundraising Techniques

1. The exception to this statement would include self-financed millionaires.

2. We constructed a measure that sums up the number of types of groups to which the donor belonged. This is different from a count of the number of groups. For example, among those who checked that they belonged to a Christian conservative group could be one donor who belonged only to the Christian Coalition and another who belonged not only to the Coalition, but also to Focus on the Family, Concerned Women for America, and the Family Research Council.

3. See Long and Freese 2001 for information on ordered probit analysis. See the Appendix for a discussion of the methodology.

4. Those who refused to answer the income question also receive more solicitations (our analysis suggests that these individuals are likely to be high-income respondents).

5. The effects were calculated by setting all of the variables at their indicated levels (and all other variables at their means) for each hypothetical individual and then calculating the difference between them. The individual effects of each of the variables in table 4.1 are presented in Appendix A-1. For a complete discussion of how to compute estimated probabilities, see Tomz, Wittenberg, King (2001) and King, Tomz, and Wittenberg (2000).

6. This contrast is between individuals comprising the top and bottom deciles on purposive motives.

7. See the Appendix for a discussion of the methodology.

8. This typical donor is a habitual contributor, belongs to an average of five political groups, asks others to give, contacts an average of two to five members of Congress, and has an education that includes some graduate work. The donor earns a family income between $100,000 and $249,999, is middle-aged (about 57 years old), is male, and identifies as an Independent. The donor does not hold a political job, belong to the Evangelical Christian, Catholic, or Jewish religion, or hold strong opinions on abortion.

5. THE CONTRIBUTION

1. This is not surprising, especially because two of the questions in the table are part of the factor analysis that identified investors.

2. The total includes all House and Senate general-election candidates and all senators not up for reelection.

3. We used data on campaign contributions from the FEC and matched that information with our surveys for this analysis.

4. There are 505,155 transactions with complete information on each variable, so we are confident about even substantively small statistical relationships.

5. Rare-events logit is used to estimate models predicting extremely uncommon events. See the Appendix for a discussion of the methodology.

6. We used ordered probit because the dependent variable was ordinal and in categories. See the Appendix for a discussion of the methodology.

7. We estimated this using a survey question that asked donors how many candidates contributed in each of several dollar ranges. To calculate a total, we simply took the midpoint of the range and multiplied it by the number of contributions. Thus someone who claimed 3 contributions of less than $200 was credited with $300, since $100 is the midpoint of that range.

8. We did not include tables for Senate candidates because the small number of cases made the results tentative.

6. THE DONORS CONTACT CONGRESS

1. This generalization is drawn from the NES 1996 Post-Election Study. Respondents were asked: "During the past twelve months, have you had any contact with a member of Congress in any way?" Note that this question asked about one year, and ours asked about 2 years.

2. See table A-2 for individual effects. The effects for material, purposive, and solidary motives are based on the change in probability between donors who

had "strong" motives (defined as within the top ten percent) and those who had "weak" motives (defined as within the bottom ten percent). The effects for "number of organizations" are based on the change in probability between donors who were "highly" active (defined as within the top ten percent, or eight or more groups) and those who were not active (defined as within the bottom ten percent, or one to zero groups). The effects for age are based on the change in probability between donors who were seventy-five or older (the top ten percent) and those who were forty or under (the bottom ten percent). All other effects for remaining variables in the model reflect changes between the maximum and minimum values. For a complete discussion of how to compute estimated probabilities, see Tomz, Wittenberg, and King (2001) and King, Tomz, and Wittenberg (2000).

3. See the Appendix for a discussion of the methodology.

4. See table A-3 for individual effects. See note 2 for more information.

5. The effects for material, purposive, and solidary motives are based on the change in probability between donors who had "strong" motives (defined as within the top ten percent) and those who had "weak" motives (defined as within the bottom ten percent).

6. See the Appendix for a discussion of the methodology.

7. See note 2 for more information on the calculation of effects.

8. See note 2.

9. See note 2.

10. See note 2.

7. Congressional Donors and Campaign Reform

1. On public perceptions of corruption, see Shapiro (2002).

2. The *Washington Post* survey was conducted between 1/9 and 1/23, 1997, and included 414 cases (Morin and Brossard 1997). A survey for the Committee for Economic Development, by the Tarrance Group, showed that 15 percent of senior executives from corporations with annual revenues of $500 million or more believed the "system was broken" and 64 percent believed it had "problems." The latter survey was conducted between 9/12 and 10/10, 2000, and included 300 cases of senior corporate executives (see Committee for Economic Development 2000). The survey of congressional (and other) candidates relied on a questionnaire mailed in March 2001. The survey received responses from 552 congressional candidates, of which 332 were major-party candidates. The sample closely approximated the actual population (see Herrnson, Lay, and Stokes 2003).

3. These conclusions are based on factor analysis of the items discussed in tables 7.1 and 7.2. The analysis employed principal components extraction with a varimax rotation and mean substitution for missing data. The three factors

produced had eigenvalues greater than one and collectively explained 64 percent of the variance.

4. These conclusions are based on factor analysis of the nine items reported in table 7.4. The analysis employed principal components extraction with a direct oblimin rotation and mean substitution for missing data. The three factors produced had eigenvalues greater than one and collectively explained 67 percent of the variance.

5. Ideology was excluded from the equation because partisanship and ideology are highly correlated (pearson r = 0.73).

6. In this context, it is important to remember that the structure of the federal government gives intense minorities many opportunities to thwart the will of the majority.

References

Abramowitz, Alan I., and Jeffery A. Segal. 1992. *Senate Elections*. Ann Arbor: University of Michigan Press.

Ackerman, Bruce. 1993. "Crediting the Voters: A New Beginning for Campaign Finance." *American Prospect* 13: 71–89.

Adler, E. Scott. 2002. "New Issues, New Members: Committee Composition and the Transformation of Issue Agendas on the House Banking and Public Works Committees." In *Policy Dynamics*, edited by Frank Baumgartner and Bryan Jones. Chicago: University of Chicago Press.

Adler, E. Scott, Chariti Gent, and Cary Overmeyer. 1998. "The Home Style Homepage: Legislator Use of the World Wide Web for Constituency Contact." *Legislative Studies Quarterly* 23: 585–595.

Agresti, Alan. 1990. *Categorical Data Analysis*. New York: John Wiley and Sons.

Alexander, Herbert. 1962. *Financing the 1960 Election*. Princeton, N.J.: Citizens' Research Foundation.

——. 1966. *Financing the 1964 Election*. Princeton, N.J.: Citizens' Research Foundation.

——. 1971. *Financing the 1968 Election*. Lexington, Mass.: Heath Lexington Books.

——. 1979. *Financing the 1976 Election*. Washington, D.C.: CQ Press.

——. 1992. *Financing Politics: Money, Elections, and Political Reform*. Washington, D.C.: CQ Press.

Alexander, Herbert, and Anthony Corrado. 1994. *Financing the 1992 Election*. Armonk, N.Y.: Sharpe.

Alexander, Herbert, Eugenia Grohman, Caroline D. Jones, and Clifford Brown. 1976. *Financing the 1972 Election*. Lexington, Mass.: Heath Lexington.

Allen, Michael Patrick, and Phillip Broyles. 2000. "Campaign Finance Reform and the Presidential Contributing of Wealthy Capitalist Families." In *Political Money: Deregulating American Politics*. Stanford, Calif.: Hoover Institute, Stanford University.

Allen, Mike. 2002. "Bush Signs Campaign Bill, Hits Road to Raise Money." *Washington Post* (March 28): A1.

Alliance for Better Campaigns. 2002. Web site: www.bettercampaigns.org.

Anderson, Annelise, ed. 2000a. *Political Money: Deregulating American Politics*. Stanford, Calif.: Hoover Institute, Stanford University.

——, ed. 2000b. "Political Money: The New Prohibition." In *Political Money: Deregulating American Politics*, edited by Annelise Anderson. Stanford, Calif.: Hoover Institute, Stanford University.

Ansolabehere, Stephen, James M. Snyder, and Charles Stewart III. 2001. "Candidate Positioning in U.S. House Elections." *American Journal of Political Science* 45: 136–159.

Austen-Smith, David. 1995. "Campaign Contributions and Access." *The American Political Science Review* 89: 566–581.

Baker, Ross K. 1989. *The New Fat Cats*. New York: Twentieth Century Fund.

Baron, David P. 1994. "Electoral Competition with Informed and Uninformed Voters." *American Political Science Review* 88: 33–47.

Baumgartner, Frank R., and Beth L. Leech. 1998. *Basic Interests: The Importance of Groups in Politics and in Political Science*. Princeton, N.J.: Princeton University Press.

Berg, Larry L., Harlan Hahn, and John R. Schmidhauser. 1976. *Corruption in the American Political System*. Morristown, N.J.: General Learning Press.

Berg, Larry L., Larry L. Eastland, and Sherry B. Jaffe. 1981. "Characteristics of Large Campaign Contributors." *Social Science Quarterly* 62: 409–423.

Biersack, Robert, John C. Green, Paul S. Herrnson, Lynda Powell, and Clyde Wilcox. 1999. "Women Big Donors Mobilized in Congressional Elections," a study supported by the Joyce Foundation.

Biersack, Robert, Paul S. Herrnson, and Clyde Wilcox. 1993. "Seeds for Success: Early Money in Congressional Elections." *Legislative Studies Quarterly* 18: 535–552.

——. 1994. *Risky Business: PAC Decisionmaking in Congressional Elections*. Armonk, N.Y.: Sharpe.

——. 1999. *After the Revolution: PACs and Lobbies in the New Republican Congress*. Boston: Allyn and Bacon.

Bocskor, Nancy.1998. (Republican fundraiser, The Nancy Bocskor Company). Personal interview by authors, August 1.

Bonifaz, John C., Gregory G. Luke, and Brenda Wright. 2001. "A Legal Strategy for Challenging *Buckley v. Valeo*." In *Superintending Democracy*, edited by Christopher P. Banks and John C. Green. Akron, Ohio: University of Akron Press.

Box-Steffensmeier, Janet M. 1996. "A Dynamic Analysis of The Role of War Chests in Campaign Strategy." *American Journal of Political Science* 40: 352–371.

Box-Steffensmeier, Janet M., J. Tobin Grant, and Thomas J. Rudolph. 2002. "The Sound with No Fury: The Effects of Campaign Finance Attitudes on

Turnout and Vote Choice in the 2000 Election." Paper delivered at Weisberg Conference.

Brookings Institution. 2002. *A Guide to the Current Congressional Campaign Finance Debate*. Web site: www.brook.edu/dybdocroot/GS/CF/debate.

Brown, Clifford W., Lynda W. Powell, and Clyde Wilcox. 1995. *Serious Money: Fundraising and Contributing in Presidential Nomination Campaigns*. New York: Cambridge University Press.

Brown, Clifford, Jr., Roman Hedges, and Lynda W. Powell. 1980a. "Modes of Elite Political Participation: Contributors to the 1972 Presidential Candidates." *American Journal of Political Science* 24: 259–290.

——. 1980b. "Belief Structure in a Political Elite: Contributors to the 1972 Presidential Candidates." *Polity* 13: 134–146.

Burrell, Barbara. 1994. *A Woman's Place is in the House*. Ann Arbor: University of Michigan Press.

Campaign Finance Institute. 2002. *Campaign Finance eGuide*. Web site: *www.cfinst.org/eguide*.

Canon, David T. 1990. *Actors, Athletes, and Astronauts: Political Amateurs in the United States Congress*. Chicago: University of Chicago Press.

Cantor, David. 1999. "The Sierra Club Political Committee." In *After the Revolution: PACs and Lobbies in the New Republican Congress*, edited by Robert Biersack, Paul S. Herrnson, and Clyde Wilcox. Boston: Allyn and Bacon.

Center for Responsive Politics. 1997. "Money and Politics Survey." Princeton Survey Research Associates. Archived at the Roper Center.

Clark, Peter, and James Q. Wilson. 1961. "Incentive System: A Theory of Organization." *Administrative Science Quarterly* 6: 129–166.

Clawson, Dan, Alan Neustadtl, and Denise Scott. 1992. *Money Talks: Corporate PACs and Political Influence*. Washington D.C.: CQ Press.

Committee for Economic Development. 2000. "Senior Business Executives Back Campaign Finance Reform." Press Release, October 18 (*www.ced.org*).

Cooper, Alexandra, John C. Green, Michael Munger, Mark J. Rozell, and Clyde Wilcox. 2002. "Continuity and Change Among American Presidential Nomination Donors." Presented at the annual meeting of the Southern Political Science Association, Atlanta.

Corrado, Anthony, Tomas E. Mann, Daniel R. Ortiz, Trevor Potter, and Frank J. Soranf, eds. 1997. *Campaign Finance Reform: A Sourcebook*. Washington, D.C.: Brookings Institution.

Costantini, Edmond, and Joel King. 1982. "Checkbook Democrats and Their Copartisans." *American Politics Quarterly* 10: 65–92.

Dabelko, Kristen La Cour, and Paul S. Herrnson. 1997. "Women and Men's Campaigns for the U.S. House of Representatives." *Political Research Quarterly* 50: 121–135.

Davidson, Roger H., and Walter J. Oleszek. 2002. *Congress and Its Members*. 8th ed. Washington D.C.: CQ Press.

Day, Christine L., Charles D. Hadley, and Megan Duffy Brown. 2001. "Gender,

Feminism, and Partisanship among Women's PAC Contributors." *Social Science Quarterly* 82: 687–701.

Deering, Christopher J., and Steven S. Smith. 1997. *Committees in Congress* 3rd ed. Washington, D.C.: CQ Press.

Delay, Tom. 2001. "Bill Jeopardizes Freedom." April 13. Web site: http://www.majoritywhip.gov/News.asp?FormMode=SingleOpEds.

Domhoff, G. William. 1983. *Who Rules America Now?: A View For the '80s*. Englewood Cliffs, N.J.: Prentice-Hall.

———. 1998. *Who Rules America? Power and Politics in the Year 2000*. New York: McGraw-Hill.

Drew, Elizabeth. 1983. *Politics and Money: The New Road to Corruption*. New York: Macmillan.

Dulio, David A., Donald L. Goff, and James A. Thurber. 1999. "Untangled Web: Internet Use During the 1998 Election." *PS: Political Science and Politics*: 53–55.

Dunn, Delmer D. 1972. *Financing Presidential Campaigns*. Washington, D.C.: Brookings Institution.

Dwyre, Diana, and Victoria A. Farrar-Meyers. 2000. *Legislative Labyrinth: Congress and Campaign Finance Reform*. Washington, D.C.: CQ Press.

Eismeier, Theodore J., and Philip H. Pollock III. 1986. "Strategy and Choice in Congressional Elections: The Role of Political Action Committees." *American Journal of Political Science* 30: 197–213.

———. 1988. *Business, Money, and the Rise of Corporate PACs in American Elections*. New York: Quorum.

Erikson, Robert, and Kent Tedin. 2000. *American Public Opinion: Its Origin, Contents, and Impact*. 6th ed. New York: Longman.

Feingold, Russ. 2001. "Opening Statement of U.S. Senator Russ Feingold on S. 27, the McCain-Feingold-Cochran Campaign Finance Reform Bill from the Floor of the United States Senate." See: http://www.senate.gov/~Efeingold/releases/01/03/20001319957.html.

Fenno, Richard F., Jr. 1978. *Home Style: House Members in their Districts*. Boston: Little, Brown.

Ferguson, Thomas. 1995. *Golden Rule: The Investment Theory of Party Competition and the Logic of Money-Driven Political Systems*. Chicago: University of Chicago Press.

Fiorina, Morris P. 1974. *Representatives, Roll Calls, and Constituencies*. Lexington, Mass.: Lexington Books.

Fowler, Linda L., and Ronald G. Shaiko. 1987. "The Grass Roots Connection: Environmental Activists and Senate Roll Calls." *American Journal of Political Science* 31: 484–510.

Francia, Peter L. 2001. "Early Fundraising by Nonincumbent Female Congressional Candidates: The Importance of Women's PACs." *Women and Politics* 23: 7–20.

Francia, Peter L., Rachel E. Goldberg, John C. Green, Paul S. Herrnson, and

Clyde Wilcox. 1999. "Individual Donors in the 1996 Federal Elections." In *Financing the 1996 Election*, edited by John C. Green. Armonk, N.Y.: Sharpe.

Francia, Peter L., and Paul S. Herrnson. 2001. "Begging for Bucks." *Campaigns & Elections* (April): 51–52.

Fuchs, Lawrence H. 1980. *The Political Behavior of American Jews*. Westport, Conn.: Greenwood.

Gierzynski, Anthony. 2000. *Money Rules: Financing Elections in America*. Boulder, Colo.: Westview.

Godwin, R. Kenneth. 1988. *One Billion Dollars of Influence: The Direct Marketing of Politics*. Chatham, N.J.: Chatham House.

Gopoian, J. David. 1984. "What Makes PACs Tick? An Analysis of the Allocation Patterns of Economic Interest Groups." *American Journal of Political Science* 28: 259–281.

Gora, Joel M. 2001. "Dollars and Sense: In Praise of *Buckley v. Valeo*," In *Superintending Democracy*, edited by Christopher P. Banks and John C. Green. Akron, Ohio: University of Akron Press.

Green, Donald Philip, and Jonathan S. Krasno. 1988. "Salvation for the Spendthrift Incumbent: Reestimating the Effects of Campaign Spending in House Elections." *American Journal of Political Science* 32: 884–907.

Green, John C., and James L. Guth. 1986. "Big Bucks and Petty Cash: Party and Interest Group Activists in American Politics." In *Interest Group Politics*, edited by Allan Cigler and Burgett Loomis. 2nd ed. Washington, D.C.: CQ Press.

——. 1988. "The Christian Right in the Republican Party: The Case of Pat Robertson's Supporters." *Journal of Politics* 50:150–165.

——. 1991. "Who is Right and Who is Left: Varieties of Ideology among Political Contributors." In *Do Elections Matter?*, edited by Benjamin Ginsberg and Alan Stone. 2d ed. Armonk, N.Y.: Sharpe.

Green, John C., John S. Jackson, and Nancy L. Clayton. 1999. "Issue Networks and Party Elites in 1996," In *The State of the Parties*, edited by John C. Green and Daniel M. Shea. 3rd ed. Lanham, Md.: Rowman & Littlefield.

Grenzke , Janet M. 1989. "PACs and the Congressional Supermarket: The Currency is Complex." *American Journal of Political Science* 33: 1–24.

Heard, Alexander. 1960. *The Costs of Democracy*. Chapel Hill: University of North Carolina Press.

Hedges, Roman. 1984. "Reasons for Political Involvement: A Study of Contributors to the 1972 Presidential Campaign." *Western Politics Quarterly* 37: 257–271.

Herndon, James F. 1982. "Access, Record, and Competition as Influences on Interest Group Contributions to Congressional Campaigns." *Journal of Politics* 44: 996–1019.

Herrnson, Paul S. 1988. *Party Campaigning in the 1980s*. Cambridge, Mass.: Harvard University Press.

——. 1989. "National Party Decision Making, Strategies, and Resource Distribution in Congressional Elections," *Western Political Quarterly* 42: 301–323.

——. 1992. "Campaign Professionalism and Fundraising in Congressional Elections." *Journal of Politics* 54: 859–870.

——. 2000. *Congressional Elections: Campaigning at Home and in Washington*, 3rd ed. Washington, D.C.: CQ Press.

Herrnson, Paul S., Celeste Lay, and Atiya Kai Stokes. 2003. "Women Running 'as Women': Candidate Gender, Campaign Issues, and Voter Targeting Strategies." *Journal of Politics*, forthcoming.

Humphries, Craig. 1991. "Corporations, PACs, and the Strategic Link between Contributions and Lobbying Activities." *Western Political Quarterly* 44: 357–372.

Jackson, Brooks. 1988. *Honest Graft*. Washington D. C.: Farragut Publishing.

Jacobson, Gary C. 1980. *Money in Congressional Elections*. New Haven: Yale University Press.

——. 1985. "Party Organization and Distribution of Campaign Resources: Republicans and Democrats in 1982." *Political Science Quarterly* 100: 603–625.

——. 2001. *The Politics of Congressional Elections*. 5th ed. New York: Longman.

Jelen, Ted, and Clyde Wilcox. 2002. "Polls and Paradoxes: Public Opinion on Abortion." Presented at the annual meeting of the American Political Science Association, Boston.

Jones, Jeffrey M. 2002. "Seven in Ten Support New Campaign Finance Legislation." Web site: www.gallup.com/poll/releases/pr020213.asp.

Jones, Ruth, and Warren Miller. 1985. "Financing Campaigns: Macro Level Innovation and Micro Level Response." *Western Politics Quarterly* 38: 187–210.

Kahn, Kim Fridkin, and Patrick J. Kenney. 1997. "A Model of Candidate Evaluations in Senate Elections: The Impact of Campaign Intensity." *The Journal of Politics* 59: 1173–1205.

——. 1999. *The Spectacle of U.S. Senate Campaigns*. Princeton: Princeton University Press.

Kazee, Thomas A., ed. 1994. *Who Runs for Congress?: Ambition, Context, and Candidate Emergence*. Washington, D.C.: CQ Press.

King, Gary, Michael Tomz, and Jason Wittenberg. 2000. "Making the Most of Statistical Analyses: Improving Interpretation and Presentation." *American Journal of Political Science* 44: 347–61.

King, Gary, and Langche Zeng. 1999. *Logistic Regression in Rare Events Data*. Cambridge, Mass.: Society for Political Methodology, Harvard University.

——. 2001. "Logistic Regression in Rare Events Data." *Political Analysis* 9: 1–27.

Kline, Paul. 2000. *A Pyschometrics Primer*. New York: Free Association.

Krasno, Jonathan S., Donald Philip Green, and Jonathan A. Cowden. 1994. "The Dynamics of Campaign Fundraising in House Elections." *Journal of Politics* 56: 459–474.

Langbein, Laura I. 1986. "Money and Access: Some Empirical Evidence." *Journal of Politics* 48: 1052–1062.

Layman, Geoffrey. 2001. *The Great Divide: Religious and Cultural Conflict in American Party Politics.* New York: Columbia University Press.

Levick-Segnatelli, Barbara. 1994. "The Washington PAC: One Man Can Make A Difference." In *Risky Business: PAC Decisionmaking in Congressional Elections,* edited by Robert Biersack, Paul S. Herrnson, and Clyde Wilcox. Armonk, N.Y.: Sharpe.

Long, J. Scott and Jeremy Freese. 2001. *Review of Regression Models for Categorical Dependent Variables Using Stata.* College Station, Tex.: Stata Corporation.

Lorr, Maurice. 1987. *Cluster Analysis for Social Scientists.* San Francisco: Josey Bass.

Magleby, David B., and Candice J. Nelson. 1990. *The Money Chase: Congressional Campaign Finance Reform.* Washington, D.C.: Brookings Institution.

Maisel, L. Sandy, Walter J. Stone, and Cherie Maestas. 2001. "Quality Challengers to Congressional Incumbents: Can Better Candidates Be Found?" In *Playing Hardball: Campaigning for the U.S. Congress,* edited by Paul S. Herrnson. New York: Prentice Hall.

Malbin, Michael J., and Thomas L. Gais. 1998. *The Day After Reform: Sobering Campaign Finance Lessons from the American States.* Albany, N.Y.: Rockefeller Institute.

McCain, John. 2002. "McCain Lauds Senate Passage of Landmark Campaign Finance Reform Bill." Press release. See: http://mccain.senate.gov/cfrpassage.htm.

McChesney, Fred S. 1997. *Money for Nothing: Politicians, Rent Extraction, and Political Extortion.* Cambridge, Mass.: Harvard University Press.

Meehan, Martin. 2002. "Time to Kick the Soft Money Habit," February 28. See: http:www.house.gov/apps/list/press/ma05_meehan/NRCFROpEd022802.html.

Meirowitz, Adam, and Alan Wiseman. 2001. "Contributions and Elections with Network Externalities." Unpublished manuscript.

Milbank, Dana. 2002. "Tactics and Theatrics Color Decision Day." *Washington Post* (February 14): A01.

Miller, Warren E., and National Election Studies / Center for Political Studies. 1979. American National Election Study, 1978. 2d ICPSR ed. Ann Arbor, Mich.: Interuniversity Consortium for Political and Social Research.

Mills, C. Wright. 1956. *The Power Elite.* New York: Oxford University Press.

Morin, Richard, and Mario A. Brossard. 1997. "Give and Take: What the Donors Really Want." *Washington Post National Weekly Edition* (February 17): 9–10.

Mundo, Philip A. 1999. "League of Conservation Voters." In *After the Revolution: PACs and Lobbies in the New Republican Congress,* edited by Robert Biersack, Paul S. Herrnson, and Clyde Wilcox. Boston: Allyn and Bacon.

Mutch, Robert E. 1988. *Campaigns, Congress, and Courts: The Making of Federal Campaign Finance Law.* New York: Praeger.

——. 1999. "AT &T PAC: The Perils of Pragmatism." In *After the Revolution:*

PACs and Lobbies in the New Republican Congress, edited by Robert Biersack, Paul S. Herrnson, and Clyde Wilcox. Boston: Allyn and Bacon.

Nelson, Candice J. and Robert Biersack. 1999. "Working to Keep a Pro-Business Congress," In *After the Revolution: PACs and Lobbies in the New Republican Congress*, edited by Robert Biersack, Paul S. Herrnson, and Clyde Wilcox. Boston: Allyn and Bacon.

Nichols, David. 1974. *Financing Elections: The Politics of an American Ruling Class.* New York: New Viewpoints.

Olson, Mancur. 1971. *The Logic of Collective Action: Public Goods and the Theory of Groups.* Cambridge, Mass.: Harvard University Press.

O'Rourke, P.J. 1990. *Parliament of Whores: A Lone Humorist Attempts to Explain the Entire U.S. Government.* New York: Atlantic Monthly Press.

Overacker, Louise. 1932. *Money in Elections.* New York: Macmillan.

Patterson, Kelly D. 1999. "Political Firepower: The National Rifle Association." In *After the Revolution: PACs and Lobbies in the New Republican Congress*, edited by Robert Biersack, Paul S. Herrnson, and Clyde Wilcox. Boston: Allyn and Bacon.

Powell, Eleanor N., Lynda W. Powell, Randall K. Thomas, and Clyde Wilcox. 2001. "Casting a Broader Net? Fundraising and Contributing through the Internet in the 2000 Presidential Election." Presented at the annual meeting of the American Political Science Association, San Francisco, Calif.

Powell, Lynda W. 1979. "A Study of Financial Contributors in Congressional Elections." Presented at the annual meeting of the American Political Science Association, Washington, D.C.

———. 1980. "A Study of Financial Contributors in Congressional Elections." Presented at the Conference on Congressional Elections, Houston, Tex.

———. 1982. "Issue Representation in Congress." *Journal of Politics* 44: 658–678.

———. 1989. "Analyzing Misinformation: Perceptions of Congressional Candidates' Ideologies." *American Journal of Political Science* 33: 272–293.

[*Record*]. 2002. "Paying for Power." *The Record* (June 16): A1.

Rosenstone, Steven J., Donald R. Kinder, Warren E. Miller, and the National Election Studies. 1997. National Election Studies, 1996: Pre- and Post-Election Study. 3d release. Ann Arbor, Mich.: University of Michigan, Center for Political Studies.

Rosenstone, Steven J., and John Mark Hansen. 1993. *Mobilization, Participation, and Democracy in America.* New York: Macmillan.

Rozell, Mark J. 1999. "WISH LIST: Pro-Choice Women in the Republican Congress." In *After the Revolution: PACs and Lobbies in the New Republican Congress*, edited by Robert Biersack, Paul S. Herrnson, and Clyde Wilcox. Boston: Allyn and Bacon.

Sabato, Larry. 1984. *PAC Power: Inside the World of Political Action Committees.* New York: Norton.

———. 1989. *Paying for Elections: The Campaign Finance Thicket.* New York: The Twentieth Century Fund.

Schattschneider, E.E. 1960. *The Semi-Sovereign People.* New York: Holt, Rinehart, and Winston.

Schlesinger, Joseph A. 1985. "The New American Political Party." *American Political Science Review* 79: 1152–1169.

Scott, Kimberly. 1999. [President of Conklin Scott.] Personal interview by authors, January 22.

Shafer, Byron E., and William Claggett. 1995. *The Two Majorities: The Issue Context of Modern American Politics.* Baltimore: Johns Hopkins University Press.

Shapiro, Robert Y. 2002. "Public Opinion and Campaign Finance." Expert report prepared for *McConnell v. FEC,* September 18.

Shays, Christopher. 2002. "Shays' Statement on the Successful Discharge Petition for the Bipartisan Campaign Reform Act." Press release, January 24.

Sinclair, Barbara. 2000. *Unorthodox Lawmaking: New Legislative Processes in the U.S. Congress,* 2d ed. Washington, D.C.: CQ Press.

Smith, Bradley A. 2000. "Campaign Finance Regulation: Faculty Assumptions and Undemocratic Consequences." In *Political Money: Deregulating American Politics,* edited by Annelise Anderson. Stanford, Calif.: Hoover Institute, Stanford University.

———. 2001. *Unfree Speech: The Folly of Campaign Finance Reform.* New Haven: Yale University Press.

Sniderman, Paul M., Richard A. Brody, and Philip E. Tetlock. 1991. *Reasoning and Choice: Explorations in Political Psychology.* Cambridge: Cambridge University Press.

Snyder, James M. 1990. "Campaign Contributions as Investments." *Journal of Political Economy* 98: 1195–1227.

Sorauf, Frank J. 1988. *Money in American Elections.* Boston: Little Brown.

———. 1992. *Inside Campaign Finance: Myths and Realities.* New Haven: Yale University Press.

———. 1999. "What Buckley Wrought," In *If Buckley Fell,* edited by Joshua E. Rosenkranz. New York: Century Foundation Press.

Stern, Philip M. 1988. *The Best Congress Money Can Buy.* New York: Random House.

Thayer, George. 1974. *Who Shakes the Money Tree?* New York: Simon and Schuster.

Thomas, Sue. 1994. "The National Abortion Rights Action League PAC: Reproductive Choice in the Spotlight." In *Risky Business: PAC Decisionmaking in Congressional Elections,* edited by Robert Biersack, Paul S. Herrnson, and Clyde Wilcox. Armonk, N.Y.: Sharpe.

———. 1999. "NARAL PAC: Battling for Women's Reproductive Rights," In *After the Revolution: PACs and Lobbies in the New Republican Congress,* edited by Robert Biersack, Paul S. Herrnson, and Clyde Wilcox. Boston: Allyn and Bacon.

Tomz, Michael, Jason Wittenberg, and Gary King. 2001. CLARIFY: Software for Interpreting and Presenting Statistical Results. Version 2.0. Cambridge, Mass.: Harvard University, June 1. See: http://gking.harvard.edu/

Verba, Sidney, Kay Lehman Schlozman, and Henry E. Brady. 1995. *Voice and Equality*. Cambridge: Harvard University Press.

Wald, Kenneth. 2003. *Religion in American Politics*, 3d ed. Lanham, Md.: Rowman and Littlefield.

Wayne, Stephen J. 1998. "Interest Groups on the Road to the White House: Traveling the Hard and Soft Routes." In *The Interest Group Connection: Electioneering, Lobbying, and Policymaking in Washington*, edited by Paul S. Herrnson, Ronald G. Shaiko, and Clyde Wilcox. New York: Seven Bridges Press.

Webster, Benjamin A., Clyde Wilcox, Paul S. Herrnson, Peter L. Francia, John C. Green, and Lynda Powell. 2001. "Competing for Cash: The Individual Financiers of Congressional Elections." In *Playing Hardball: Campaigning for the U.S. Congress*, edited by Paul S. Herrnson. Upper Saddle River, N.J.: Prentice Hall.

West, Darrell M., and John M. Orman. 2003. *Celebrity Politics*. Upper Saddle River, N.J.: Prentice Hall.

Westle, Mark C. 1991. *Senate Elections and Campaign Intensity*. Baltimore: Johns Hopkins University Press.

Wilcox, Clyde. 2001. "Contributing as Participation." In *A User's Guide to Campaign Finance Reform*, edited by Jerry Lubenow. Lanham, Md.: Rowman & Littlefield.

Wilcox, Clyde, Robert Biersack, Paul S. Herrnson, and Wesley Joe. 1998. "Contribution Strategies of Large Congressional Donors: 1978–1994." Los Angeles: Citizens' Research Foundation.

Wilcox, Clyde, John C. Green, Paul S. Herrnson, Peter L. Francia, Lynda W. Powell, and Benjamin A. Webster. 2002. "Raising the Limits: Campaign Finance Reform May Hold Some Surprises." *Public Perspective*, May/June: 11–15.

Wilson, James Q. 1973. *Political Organizations*. Princeton: Princeton University Press.

Winter, Ralph K. 1973. *Campaign Financing and Political Freedom*. Washington, D.C.: American Enterprise Institute.

Index

John G. Geer, *From Tea Leaves to Opinion Polls: A Theory of Democratic Leadership*

Kim Fridkin Kahn, *The Political Consequences of Being a Woman: How Stereotypes Influence the Conduct and Consequences of Political Campaigns*

Kelly D. Patterson, *Political Parties and the Maintenance of Liberal Democracy*

Dona Cooper Hamilton and Charles V. Hamilton, *The Dual Agenda: Race and Social Welfare Policies of Civil Rights Organizations*

Hanes Walton Jr., *African-American Power and Politics: The Political Context Variable*

Amy Fried, *Muffled Echoes: Oliver North and the Politics of Public Opinion*

Russell D. Riley, *The Presidency and the Politics of Racial Inequality: Nation-Keeping from 1831 to 1965*

Robert W. Bailey, *Gay Politics, Urban Politics: Identity and Economics in the Urban Setting*

Ronald T. Libby, *ECO-WARS: Political Campaigns and Social Movements*

Donald Grier Stephenson Jr., *Campaigns and the Court: The U.S. Supreme Court in Presidential Elections*

Kenneth Dautrich and Thomas H. Hartley, *How the News Media Fail American Voters: Causes, Consequences, and Remedies*

Douglas C. Foyle, *Counting the Public In: Presidents, Public Opinion, and Foreign Policy*

Ronald G. Shaiko, *Voices and Echoes for the Environment: Public Interest Representation in the 1990s and Beyond*

Hanes Walton Jr., *Reelection: William Jefferson Clinton as a Native-Son Presidential Candidate*

Demetrios James Caraley, editor, *The New American Interventionism: Lessons from Successes and Failures—Essays from* Political Science Quarterly

Ellen D. B. Riggle and Barry L. Tadlock, editors, *Gays and Lesbians in the Democratic Process: Public Policy, Public Opinion, and Political Representation*

Robert Y. Shapiro, Martha Joynt Kumar, Lawrence R. Jacobs, Editors, *Presidential Power: Forging the Presidency for the Twenty-First Century*

Kerry L. Haynie, *African American Legislators in the American States*

Marissa Martino Golden, *What Motivates Bureaucrats? Politics and Administration During the Reagan Years*

Geoffrey Layman, *The Great Divide: Religious and Cultural Conflict in American Party Politics*

Sally S. Cohen, *Championing Child Care*

Judith Russell, *Economics, Bureaucracy, and Race: How Keynesians Misguided the War on Poverty*

DATE DUE

Demco, Inc. 38-293